Storm Across Asia

Genghis Khan and the Mongols

The Mogul Expansion

Imperial Visions

The Rise and Fall of Empires

Storm Across Asia

Genghis Khan and the Mongols

The Mogul Expansion

Henry Wiencek
Genghis Khan and the Mongols

Glenn D. Lowry
with Amanda Heller
The Mogul Expansion

Preface by W. M. Thackston, Jr.
Associate Professor of Persian
Harvard University

HBJ Press
a subsidiary of Harcourt Brace Jovanovich
New York, New York

HBJ Press

Publisher, John R. Whitman
Executive Editor, Marcia Heath
Managing Editor, Janice Lemmo
Series Editors: John Radziewicz, Suzanne Stewart
Editorial Production, Hope Keller

Marketing Staff: Mark A. Mayer, Jose J. Elizalde, Laurie Farber

Authors: Henry Wiencek, Glenn D. Lowry, Amanda Heller
Picture Researcher, Janet Adams
Assistant Picture Researcher, Lynn Bowdery

Historical Consultant, Kenneth Maxwell

Design Implementation, Designworks

Rizzoli Editore

Authors of the Italian Edition
    Introduction: Professor Ovidio Dallera
    Genghis Khan and the Mongols: Drs. Ada and Alberto
      Vacchi
    The Mogul Expansion: Dr. Sergio Stocchi
    Maps: Gian Franco Leonardi
Idea and Realization, Harry C. Lindinger
Graphic Design, Gerry Valsecchi
General Editorial Supervisor, Ovidio Dallera

Library of Congress Cataloging in Publication Data
Main entry under title:
Storm across Asia.

    (Imperial visions ; v. 7)
    Includes index.
    CONTENTS: Wiencek, H.   Genghis Khan and the
Mongols.—Lowry, G. D., and Heller, A.   The Mogul
expansion.
    1. Mongols—History   I. Wiencek, Henry.
Genghis Khan and the Mongols. 1980   II. Lowry,
Glenn D.   The Mogul expansion. 1980.   III. Series.
DS19.S82   950′.2   79-2519
ISBN 0-15-004029-6

Contents

Preface

Before the age of discovery and global awareness, contacts between Europeans and the peoples of central Asia and the Indian subcontinent were few and isolated. Two of the peoples in this vast region to leave a lasting mark on Western consciousness are the Mongols and the Moguls. Both of these names still conjure vivid images in the mind. The Mongols evoke dread and fear—Slavs still pray in their litanies that God will preserve them from the "wrath of the Tatar"—and the Moguls of India, distant kindred of the Mongols, have lent their name to autocratic potentates and to anything grandiose or lavish. Both peoples founded empires by force of conquest and long after assimilation to their subject peoples in most facets of life maintained institutions derived from the nomadic traditions of the central Asian steppe, such as land tenure based on military patronage and a preference for highly mobile courts over fixed capital cities.

In the first half of the thirteenth century, mention of the Mongol hordes—the "Scourge of God"—could cause trepidation from the Atlantic to the Pacific. Some attempted valiantly but vainly to resist the Mongols, while others resigned themselves to their doom at the hands of what were considered instruments of God's punishment for the sins of mankind. Those who experienced firsthand the wrath of the invading armies indeed had cause for alarm. Having relatively few fighting men for an all-conquering army and lacking the experience and will to administer vast regions of settled peoples, the Mongols elected to destroy as a matter of course what was not perceived by them to be of immediate benefit. Only after the breakup of the unified empire of Genghis Khan and his sons did the Mongols begin to see the advantage of proper administration.

Although the cultural level of the Mongols themselves was abysmally low in comparison to that of the Chinese and Persians they conquered, all the havoc and destruction wrought by the "apes of saddles" (to quote an Arab poet of Baghdad) did not bring civilization to a halt, as had been predicted; in fact, an unprecedented cultural flowering took place in Mongol-governed China and Iran. Under the patronage of Mongol rulers, who were rapidly assimilated into the cultural milieu of their subject peoples, artists created what became classic norms of literature, painting, and architecture. The concurrent resurgence of interest in mysticism in both Europe and the Islamic world during the thirteenth century may have had its nascence in a turning inward to escape the all-too-real physical threat of the Mongols. In the economic prosperity and social revival that followed, mysticism and mystically tinged literature continued to flourish, especially in the Iranian world.

Quite different from the devastating onslaught of the Mongols was the arrival of the Moguls in India. Zahir ud-Din Mohammed Baber, a descendant of Genghis Khan, brought his followers from their ancestral home of Transoxiana in central Asia into the Indus Valley, where they found a Moslem ruling elite that had adopted many of their cultural notions wholesale from the Persianate literary culture of Iran—as the Moguls themselves had done. Baber and his son Humayun initially represented little more than two in a long series of foreign rulers from the north who had successively assumed a tenuous control over northern India. Under Akbar and his successors, though, the empire expanded to include the greater part of the subcontinent, in part because of a shrewd alliance with the militant Rajput warrior-princes.

More important, the dominant Persianizing cultural modes, fed by a constant influx of talent from Safawid Iran, were synthesized with native Indian elements during the Mogul period to create a vibrant grace and refinement bolstered by practically limitless wealth. Under Mogul patronage, the arts attained a technical perfection that was uniquely Mogul in style and conceptualization and rarely rivaled in all of Islamic civilization. Unfortunately, the empire was unable to create a society as integrated as its arts or to deal successfully with the tensions it had created, and it soon crumbled politically; the pieces were subsequently gathered by the British and incorporated into their Indian Empire. Still, the legacy that the Moguls bequeathed to India in literature, music, architecture, and painting remains one of the most notable achievements of world civilization.

W. M. THACKSTON, JR.
Associate Professor of Persian
Harvard University

Genghis Khan and
the Mongols

In the winter of 1206, the treasurers of the emperor of North China reported that one of the empire's less important vassals, the Mongol khan, had neglected to pay the annual tribute required of a loyal subject. A prince was dispatched to find the camp of the Mongols—somewhere in "the distant land" north of the Gobi Desert—and collect the payment, but there was little anxiety at the Peking court. The Chinese had defeated Mongol bands before and had managed to keep them in a state of powerless disunity. Indeed, the Mongols were despised by other nomadic tribes for their poverty and ignorance: They had no wealth aside from their horses and sheep, made nothing worth trading with foreigners, and, unlike their more

Preceding page, a yurt, or Mongol tent. Made of felt stretched over a frame of wooden slats, the yurt of today differs little from that of Genghis Khan's time—eight hundred years ago—when it was the only means of shelter for the nomadic Mongols.

Above, a landscape in Mongolia. High mountain ranges—the Altai and the Khangai—alternating with steppe that averages over 5,200 feet in altitude shield much of the terrain. Some mountain peaks soar to 13,000 feet above sea level. Lake Baikal (right), which formed a part of the Mongol realm, is now under Soviet control.

civilized Turkish neighbors, could not read or write.

As the Chinese prince was making his way north, he was surprised to encounter Turks and Mongols from as far east as the Khingan Mountains and as far west as the Altai Mountains also heading for the khan's headquarters. His apprehension grew when he reached the camp and saw the tent of the chief, Genghis Khan, decorated with fine brocades and gold plaques. The khan handed over the usual gifts and hurried the prince on his way back to Peking. Once in Peking, the prince's warnings about the new wealth and power of the Mongols were dismissed. The emperor felt secure behind the thirteen-hundred-year-old Great Wall, and his chief commander asserted that all was quiet among the roaming tribesmen of the north.

The calm that prevailed among the northern

tribesmen had been achieved only after two decades of wars waged by Genghis Khan to bring under his sway "all the people who dwell in felt tents." Genghis Khan assembled the tribes in 1206 so that he could publicly proclaim a nation called "The Blue Mongols," under the protection of the heavenly sky. Before the gathering of princes he recounted the deeds of his warriors, praised those who had been loyal to him, promulgated a system of laws by which he would govern, and selected a "bodyguard"—an army

Above, part of a herd of cattle in Mongolia today. The descendants of Genghis Khan make their living largely from herding, as did their ancestors centuries ago.

Above right, a scene in Mongolia, showing in the background the yurts used for shelter on the steppe. Right, a steppe landscape.

of ten thousand men. Privately, he revealed his intention of invading China, not on a hasty raid for plunder but on a prolonged expedition of conquest.

Genghis Khan did not then foresee that he would set in motion a machine of conquest that would establish the largest empire in history. In the next century, Mongol warriors would invade Japan, come within sixty miles of Venice, impose their rule from Korea to Hungary, found a new dynasty in China, and create a regime in Russia that was to last over two hundred years. The Mongol Empire is remarkable for the speed of its conquest, for its size, and most of all for its unlikely creators—a confederation of

nomads from one of the most forbidding places on earth.

The homeland of the Mongols lay along the banks of the Onon River, a branch of the Amur that today forms part of the border between China and the Soviet Union. The Onon basin is rich grassland, part of the steppe that stretches from Manchuria all the way to Hungary, interrupted but not entirely blocked by the Altai Mountains of central Asia. To the south and west of the Altai are the Pamirs, the Hindu Kush, and the Himalayas, towering mountain ranges that cut off East Asia from Middle Asia. The steppe lands

These pages, some of the lands over which the Mongols of Genghis Khan held sway. Left, an Afghan valley near Bamian, a city destroyed by Genghis Khan in 1220. Above, the landscape of Georgia—now a Soviet republic between the Caucasus Mountains and Turkey—where the Mongol invasion of Europe began. Right, a river valley in Azerbaijan, Iran, a region that was a stronghold of the Mongol rule in Persia. Following pages, a view of a forbidding desert in Afghanistan, one of the natural barriers crossed by the Mongols.

where the Mongols first lived are separated from China by the Gobi Desert, where lakes and rivers have been known to dry up before the eyes of travelers and sand dunes to shift in the course of a night. Because all landmarks might disappear before daybreak, local caravan guides would lay out arrows pointing the right direction of travel before nightfall.

The steppe itself is only slightly more hospitable than the desert. Temperatures range from forty degrees below freezing in winter to over one hundred in summer—and even then bitter winds from Siberia blow down with incredible suddenness. (A European missionary who journeyed to the Mongol court in the thirteenth century wrote that the wind could almost blow a rider off his horse, and he described a hailstorm so heavy that men were drowned when the hail melted.)

The Mongols and Turks who inhabited the steppe endured a rough life as herders of sheep and cattle and breeders of horses. They were also proficient hunters but regarded hunting more as sport and training for war than as a livelihood. In fact they were contemptuous of the hunters of the Siberian forest, though their opinion of city dwellers was even lower. The Mongols moved with the seasons in search of pastures, living in tents known as yurts. The yurt was

The forerunners of the Mongols

Some six centuries before the Mongols established their empire, another people of the Asian steppe—the Turks—created a realm stretching from Mongolia to the Black Sea. This was only the first of the Turkish empires, which had a far more lasting impact on history than the Mongol Empire. (The last Turkish empire, the Ottoman, lasted until World War One.)

In the tenth century, Turkish mercenaries in the service of the Persians overthrew their masters and established the short-lived Ghaznavid Empire, which was supplanted in the eleventh century by the Seljuk Empire. (The pictures on these pages depict some of the battles of this period.) By 1055, Seljuk armies had conquered territory as far west as Baghdad, and sixteen years later they defeated the Byzantine emperor at Manzikert, winning the region now known as Turkey. The Seljuk realm, which extended from what is now western China to the Mediterranean, broke up in the twelfth century, with the regions of Persia and Khwarizm conquered by Mohammed II. This monarch provoked Genghis Khan by murdering a Mongol ambassador and lost his realm in the subsequent war of revenge.

A large part of Genghis Khan's army was composed of Turks. Because the Turks were literate and more civilized than the Mongols, they played an important part in the government of the Mongol Empire.

This page, top and bottom, Turkish troops battling each other in Khorasan early in the eleventh century, when rival factions struggled for power. The drum in the top picture was used to pace horses at the beginning of an attack. Immediately above, a Turkish general and a scribe.

Below, a cavalry battle between Turkish factions. Above and left, the siege of the fortress of Arg, near Bukhara, in 1003. The catapult in the left picture is similar to the one later used by the Mongols.

made of felt and was usually supported by wooden rods that could be taken apart quickly and packed onto wagons. (Only the chief of a tribe had a permanent tent, which could be moved intact on an enormous wagon.)

Because the Mongols lived at the mercy of their surroundings, it is not surprising that their religious practices reveal a deep respect for nature. The Mongols venerated the sky, the moon, and the stars, and they genuflected before the sun at dawn. Rivers were sacred, and the Mongols took elaborate precautions to avoid polluting them; washing or urinating in a stream, for example, was forbidden. The Mongols also revered fire as a purifying element; trash was never burned, nor could a knife be passed through a fire lest it "behead" the flames.

Below, Genghis Khan in front of a tent with some of his retainers. Born around 1167, Genghis Khan was given the name Temujin, after a Tatar chieftain his father had captured in battle. At the age of twenty-eight, Temujin was elected khan, or chief, of the Mongols and received the title Genghis ("Universal").

In every yurt there were several idols representing gods that watched over the occupants. At every meal the Mongols fed each god by rubbing meat and broth over the mouths of the idols. In number the gods were virtually infinite, signifying a universal supernatural presence. When a Moslem imam described his faith to Genghis Khan, the Mongol leader asked: "Why do you make the pilgrimage to Mecca? Do you not know that god is everywhere?"

The priests of the Mongol religion—shamans—held

Above, a portrait of Yesugai, the father of Genghis Khan. Yesugai was a prominent figure in the Mongols' wars against the Chin emperors of North China and their allies in the decades before Temujin's birth. Even after the Chinese and their allies smashed a confederation of Mongols, Yesugai was able to retain the loyalty of a few tribes until his death. Below, a Persian depiction of Mongol cavalry in action. The Mongols always fought on horseback, using bows and arrows, swords, and lances as their main weapons.

Left, the Mongol army besieging a Persian town. During Genghis Khan's wars in the Middle East, millions of soldiers and civilians were killed; many towns and farming areas did not recover from the devastation for decades. Top, the Mongol army facing an enemy force across a river on the steppe. Immediately above, a surprise attack on a camp.

a position of great honor in society. They communed with the gods and the spirits of the dead, going into trances and ecstasies during visits to heaven or the underworld. Accounts have survived of the complex rituals acted out by shamans to purify a tent after someone had died there. In the presence of the dead person's relatives the shaman entered a trance, spoke in the voice of the dead, and conducted the deceased's spirit to the underworld. Before any important undertaking the khan consulted a shaman, who would then speak with the gods and communicate their commands to the khan. The religious powers of the shamans gave them great secular authority, which Genghis Khan himself was forced to deal with head on. Once, when the chief shaman spread rumors alleging the disloyalty of the khan's brother, Genghis Khan allowed the shaman to be killed—a calculated act of sacrilege that terrified the people and symbolized Genghis Khan's absolute power.

After their conquests, the Mongols adopted the religions of their subjects—mainly Islam and Buddhism—and did not persecute any faith. The Mongols had a lively interest in the beliefs of foreigners and recognized the political advantages of religious tolerance, which was decreed by Genghis Khan's law. Visitors to the Mongol capital of Karakorum were struck by the presence of mosques, churches, and temples alongside one another.

Much of what is known about the Mongols derives from accounts written by Europeans who visited the Mongol Empire, notably Marco Polo, Giovanni de Piano Carpini, and William of Rubruck. The only Mongol sources are a history written in the seventeenth century by a man who claimed descent from Genghis Khan, and *The Secret History of the Mongols,* a thirteenth-century text that combines history with legend. In the fashion of the *Iliad* and the *Odyssey, The Secret History* chronicles the heroic exploits of Genghis Khan that were originally told around smoky dung fires in the Mongol yurts.

The legendary deeds recounted in the *The Secret History* inflamed the imagination and pride of the Mongols, convincing them that Genghis Khan was heaven-sent to unite the nomads against their enemies. Even Genghis Khan's birth, around 1167, was portentous: According to the chronicle, the future conquerer came into the world prophetically clutching a clot of black blood. His father named him Temujin, after an enemy chief he had captured in battle. As a teenager, Temujin was already a famous figure among the Mongols, reputed to have hunted down a band of thieves with only one companion and retrieved his family's stolen horses in a running battle with bow and arrow. The Mongols marveled at tales of how the youth escaped from an enemy camp with his neck locked in a wooden stock. It was even said that heaven directed a falcon to feed Temujin when

Left, stone monoliths—believed to date from the time of Genghis Khan—about one hundred miles from Ulan Bator, the capital of modern Mongolia. Below, a votive stele engraved with the name of Genghis Khan. After his death, Genghis Khan was literally idolized by many Mongols. Images of the khan were placed in tents, and foreigners who refused to pay homage to the idols were killed.

he was hiding from pursuers and that a giant rock fell into his path from nowhere when he was about to ride into an ambush.

Before he was thirty, Temujin's prowess in battle, his generosity in sharing spoils, and his shrewd diplomacy won him tens of thousands of followers. The Mongol princes chose him to be their khan, or ruler, and bestowed on him the name Genghis ("Universal"). Nonetheless, opponents of Genghis Khan's rule were numerous, and years of tribal warfare followed the election. All adversaries were subdued or dead by 1206, the year that marks the beginning of the Mongol Empire.

In 1207 a delegation from Peking again made its way to the Onon to inform Genghis Khan that a new emperor had ascended the throne of China—the prince of Wei. On hearing this, Genghis Khan stated that the emperor "must be an eminent personage, designated by heaven." He then asked: "How can an imbecile like the prince of Wei perform such a role?" Before the astonished ambassadors could make any response, the khan spat contemptuously and rode off.

The enmity between the nomads of the steppe and the farmers and traders of China dated as far back as the third century B.C., when the Chinese began to build the Great Wall along their border to keep out

These stone remains (above, in the fore-ground) in Soviet Kazakhstan are believed by some to date from the Mongol era. Right, a stone lion from the Mongols' capital of Karakorum.

raiding parties. In the tenth century, barbarians from the north known as the Khitan conquered much of North China, including Peking. The Chinese Sung emperors, forced to retreat to South China, sought the help of Juchen nomads. The Juchen ousted the Khitan but then—to the great surprise of the Sung—set themselves up as the Chin ("Golden") emperors. This was the situation in China when Genghis Khan began his invasion in 1211.

For two years the Mongol army, accustomed to battles fought on horseback in the open, was blocked by the Great Wall and had to content itself with taking border outposts. The breakthrough finally

The tent (right) of a contemporary Mongolian differs from the tent of Genghis Khan's time in only one major respect—its wooden doors. (Earlier yurts had simple flaps.) The felt tent-covering is sometimes coated with grease to keep out the wind and rain and then colored with white lime or crushed animal bones.

Below, the interior of a modern yurt. The wooden strips that support the tent can be quickly disassembled and stacked for transport. The opening at the top permits smoke from the cooking fire to escape.

The Mongols' simple shelters

The Mongols' nomadic way of life necessitated a shelter that was easily taken apart and transported but yet sturdy enough to withstand the high winds and extreme temperatures of the steppes. The yurt met all these requirements admirably: Its wooden framework was collapsible, its felt walls could be rolled up, and the entire structure could be transported handily on horses or oxen.

The Mongols had no desire to live in permanent buildings, and even after amassing great wealth through their conquests they continued to use yurts as their homes. The tents' furnishings were simple: a bed with a rough woolen mattress, animal skins for blankets, and wicker baskets lined with felt to serve as clothes chests. At the center of the yurt was the fire used for cooking; it was placed under a hole in the roof to allow the smoke to escape.

The traditional yurt has survived in Mongolia to the present day.

Above and left, two views of the sumptuously dec-orated yurts used by Mongol nobles in Genghis Khan's time. Below, a Mongolian woman and boy standing in front of a yurt. The boy's cap is re-markably similar to the one worn by ancient Mongol warriors.

In the winter of 1220, during the war against Khwarizm, Genghis Khan captured the city of Bukhara. The inhabitants surrendered and were not mistreated, though the khan did order that an enormous ransom be paid immediately in exchange for their safety. Immediately below, the ransom demand being made. Bottom, the walls of the citadel of Bukhara, where a garrison held out after the citizens of the city had capitulated. In storming the garrison, the Mongols inadvertently started fires that leveled the city. Near right, the minaret of a mosque in Bukhara.

Top right, a mausoleum built in Bukhara in the fourteenth century, when the city was reconstructed by Moslem governors installed by the Mongols. Center right, Genghis Khan haranguing the citizens of Bukhara after his victory, claiming that he represents the punishment of God for their rulers' misdeeds.

came when Genghis Khan ordered Jebe, one of his generals, to head a detachment of riders into a seventeen-mile-long gorge that led to the plain beyond the wall. Jebe charged the Chin defenders of the gorge but then suddenly retreated, luring the Chin defenders out of their positions. With the Chin troops in headlong pursuit, Jebe's shocked troops turned and charged again. At that moment, Genghis Khan appeared behind Jebe, and the Mongols routed the Chin.

This decisive victory unleashed the Mongol horde into the plains of China, where they trampled fields and pillaged towns for two years. In 1215 a Chin general went over to the Mongols and led them into Peking. At this point, Genghis Khan placed a general in charge of a series of sieges. The khan then returned to Mongolia so that he might better attend to a pressing matter in the west.

The son of one of Genghis Khan's tribal enemies had taken refuge among the Kara-Khitan, whose kingdom was in the steppe south of Lake Balkhash (now in the south-central Soviet Union). The exiled Mongol had treacherously imprisoned the king of the Kara-Khitan, placed himself on the throne, and begun oppressing the people, particularly his Moslem subjects. When the Kara-Khitan appealed for aid,

This page, three representations of Genghis Khan. Above, a fourteenth-century Persian view of a court scene. The khan here wears a long-sleeved robe so that supplicants will not actually touch him. Left, a manuscript leaf, with the khan the center figure at the bottom of the page. Below, a Chinese artist's portrait of Genghis Khan hunting with a falcon.

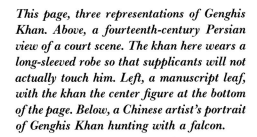

Above, a thirteenth-century Persian cup with a representation of a Mongol horseman. Right, the elevation of Temujin to Genghis Khan, as depicted in a Persian miniature.

Genghis Khan sent his trusted general Jebe, who was immediately welcomed as a savior. The gates of the capital were thrown open to Jebe, and the Kara-Khitan hunted down the supporters of the usurpers. By restraining his men from pillage and by authorizing the free practice of all religions, Jebe ingratiated himself with the local inhabitants, who gladly placed themselves under the banner of Genghis Khan.

Acquisition of the lands of the Kara-Khitan brought the Mongols in contact for the first time with the highly developed Moslem civilization of the Persians and Arabs. From the Hindu Kush to the Persian Gulf and the Caspian Sea stretched the empire of Khwarizm, one of the oldest centers of Asian civilization. Its capital, Urgench, was a seat of Moslem learning, and Samarkand was a city fabled throughout Asia for its lush gardens fed by skillfully built canals in the middle of a desert. Metals, leather, and cloth from Samarkand were prized luxuries, and the wealthy purchased Samarkand melons transported in lead casks filled with snow.

The merchants and rulers of this wealthy empire, including Shah Mohammed II, regarded the Mongols as ignorant barbarians who could easily be exploited. Khwarizmian merchants led a caravan to the encampment of Genghis Khan and brazenly over-charged him for everything he bought. To show that he had caught on to them, the khan confiscated the entire caravan—but then made amends by paying the traders even more than they had expected. The khan had an ambassador accompany the traders on their return to Khwarizm, instructing him to inform the shah: "I have the greatest desire to live in peace with you. I shall look on you as my son. . . . You know that my country is an ant heap of warriors, a mine of silver, and that I have no need to covet other dominions. We have an equal interest in fostering trade between our subjects."

To demonstrate his intentions, Genghis Khan dispatched a caravan with samples of the riches of his empire: a train of five hundred camels bearing precious metals, silk from China, and furs. In addition, the princes of the Mongol Empire each sent a personal buyer to acquire Khwarizmian goods. When the caravan reached the frontier, though, one of the shah's governors seized all the goods and put the Mongols to death. Genghis Khan, enraged, dispatched an ambassador to demand that the governor be handed over for a Mongol trial. The shah then executed the ambassador—an act the Mongols regarded as an unforgiveable atrocity, one that could be rectified only by war.

The Mongol horde that set out for the empire of Khwarizm in 1219 was a disciplined, well-drilled force, and its generals were without equals in any nation. (Though the word "horde" suggests a disorganized rabble, its root word in the Mongol language—*orda*—simply means "a camp.") Genghis Khan divided the army into decimal units. The smallest was a group of ten, and the largest a ten-thousand-man outfit. The basic weapon of every Mongol soldier was the bow and arrow, which had a range of perhaps three hundred yards. The entire army was provided with horses, and every soldier was assured a fresh mount during battle. When Mongol command-

The Mongols' war against China, launched in 1211, continued intermittently for over sixty years. Below, Mongol and Chinese cavalry fighting a battle in a mountain pass. Above right, Mongol engineers diverting a Chinese river—a tactic also used by the Mongols in their Middle Eastern wars.

Below, a Persian depiction of the Mongols besieging a Chinese city. Historians consider it unlikely, however, that the Mongols used cannons in the Chinese wars. Right, the Great Wall of China, which delayed the Mongol invasion for two years.

ers needed infantry to bear the brunt of an assault against a heavily defended bastion, they drove prisoners and civilians in front of the ranks of horsemen. Captives were also forced to fill in trenches with dirt and position siege equipment under fire.

The army's battle line was five men deep. The front two ranks were heavy cavalry—men armed with lances and wearing chest armor made of hide or pieces of iron sewn into leather. Behind them were three ranks of light cavalry wearing light leather armor. Every soldier wore a shirt of raw silk as protection against arrow wounds. An arrow would push the silk into the wound ahead of it so that a field doctor (the army was attended by Chinese and, later, Persian physicians) could dislodge the arrow by simply removing the fabric.

The Mongol's favorite tactic in a pitched battle was to send a "suicide corps" galloping toward the enemy ranks. The corps would then turn and fake a retreat to tempt the enemy into a disorganized chase. When the enemy was strung out in pursuit and their horses tired, the entire Mongol force would charge into them according to a set plan. The light cavalry would gallop back and forth pelting the enemy with arrows, after which the heavy cavalry charged in with their lances. The field commanders directed these

Genghis Khan's war against Khwarizm was a whirlwind of destruction and slaughter. Above and left, the ruins of Bamian, a city in what is now Afghanistan. A center of Buddhism, where more than one thousand monks lived in monasteries, the city fiercely resisted a Mongol siege in 1221. Genghis Khan eventually took personal control of the siege and leveled the city, which remained uninhabited for forty years. So great was the devastation that Bamian was renamed the "accursed place."

Center, above and below, the ruins of Bamian. Near left, Herat, another city in present-day Afghanistan razed by order of Genghis Khan after all its inhabitants had been slain in a week-long slaughter. Below, a battle in Khwarizm as recorded by a Persian artist.

maneuvers by means of flags, torches, and whistling arrows. Their messenger system was so efficient that armies hundreds of miles apart were able to coordinate their movements perfectly. Subotai, one of Genghis Khan's generals, was a master at mapping complex strategies involving several armies at once. Modern scholars have called his strategy for the Khwarizmian campaign one of the most brilliant in military history.

Trusting to surprise and mobility to make the difference, Subotai split the badly outnumbered Mongol forces into four armies—a southern arm, two central thrusts, and a northern flanking force. As the southern wing entered Khwarizm and engaged the shah's forces, the two center groups attacked the cities of Khojend and Otrar. Khojend fell quickly to the Mongol attackers. The defenders of Otrar, the seat of the governor who had touched off the war by slaughtering the Mongol caravan, fought fiercely, realizing they would receive no quarter. The siege of the city lasted five months, and at its end only the governor, his wife, and a few guards remained alive. The few survivors took refuge on a roof and hurled tiles on the attackers when their arrows ran out. The Mongols burrowed into the building until it collapsed and pulled the governor alive out of the rubble. As fitting punishment for his greed, the governor was put to

33

Preceding pages, the funeral procession of Genghis Khan. The khan died in August 1227, during the war against the Tangut people. To ensure the success of the Tangut campaign and to prevent uprisings in other parts of the empire, word of the khan's death was kept secret; every person who encountered the procession was killed. Genghis Khan was buried on Mount Burkan-Kaldun, but the exact location of his grave is unknown.

Above and left, views of the two unsuccessful Mongol invasions of Japan, mounted in 1274 and 1281. The first invasion force, of about 10,000 soldiers, was so poorly equipped that it lost a major battle when its supply of arrows ran out. The second invasion force, of some 140,000 men, was held to a narrow beachhead by the Japanese; after two months, its fleet of 3,500 ships was wrecked by a typhoon. The Japanese called the storm kamikaze—the divine wind—a word they used in World War Two to refer to their corps of suicide pilots. Right, a Japanese depiction of a Mongol archer and three horses.

death by having molten silver poured into his eyes and ears.

With his defensive front crumbling, the shah was attempting to rally his forces at Samarkand when the stunning news came that yet another army—Subotai's northern wing—had crossed a desert believed to be uncrossable and was besieging Bukhara, four hundred miles behind his lines to the west. Because Bukhara was not well fortified and since most of its garrison had fled as soon as the Mongols appeared, the inhabitants surrendered. Genghis Khan ordered the people to pay tribute and publicly humiliated the Moslem imams by allowing his soldiers to desecrate the mosque. The pages of the Koran were scattered about a courtyard, and the cases that had held them were used as fodder troughs for the horses. From the pulpit of the mosque, Genghis Khan told his new subjects of the provocations that had started the war, saying: "It is your leaders who have committed these crimes and I am the punishment of God." Though the khan restrained his soldiers from plundering Bukhara after the citizens had paid tribute, a fire broke out when the Mongols were rooting out the last of the garrison, and the entire city burned to the ground.

Samarkand surrendered to the Mongols after a brief siege, but the Khwarizmian capital of Urgench was defended to the bloody end by fanatical supporters of the shah. The city was set afire, house by house, and nearly all the inhabitants were slain. All over Khwarizm, towns were sacked and their inhabitants ruthlessly slaughtered, making future resistance impossible. In one instance, the Mongols slit open all the corpses of a town after one old woman admitted to having swallowed some pearls. The only people spared were artisans—metalworkers, engineers, smiths, leather workers, and others who would be useful to the khan.

After the fall of Samarkand, Mohammed abandoned his armies and took flight. On orders from Genghis Khan, Jebe and Subotai pursued the shah on an erratic course through his empire. They nearly caught up with him several times, but the shah was

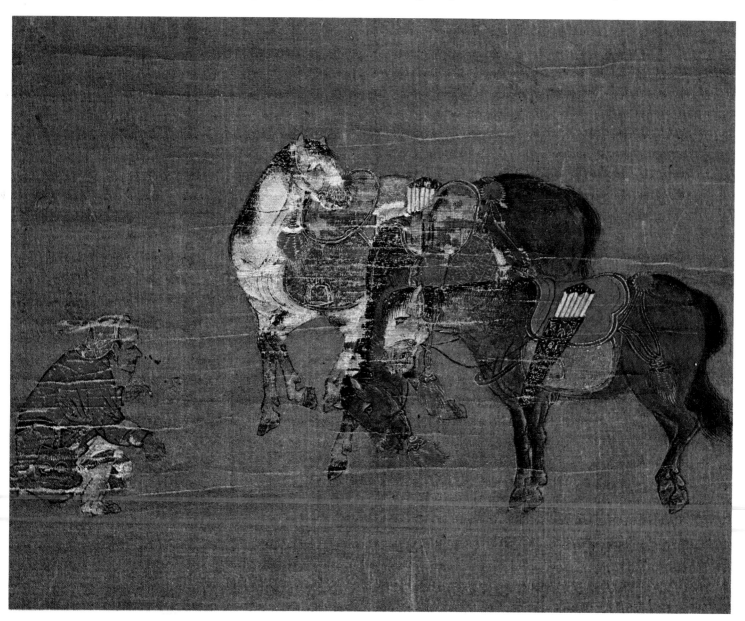

always able to make his escape. The dogged Mongols were just a few hundred yards behind him when Mohammed leaped onto a fishing boat and sailed into the Caspian Sea amid a rain of arrows. Impoverished, he died on an island shortly thereafter.

The Mongol conquest of Khwarizm, which was the crossroads of the caravan trade between medieval Europe and Asia, created a case of mistaken identity on a grand scale. In the summer of 1221, the bishop of Acre on the coast of Palestine dispatched a letter about the war in Khwarizm to Pope Honorius III that sent jubilation throughout Europe. The bishop was an ardent supporter of the Third Crusade, then being waged against the sultan of Egypt, and his letter announced the arrival of an unexpected ally: "A new and mighty protector of Christianity has arisen.

King David of India, at the head of an army of unparalleled size, has taken the field against the unbelievers." The letter went on to say that King David had already destroyed the Moslem realm in Persia and was only a few days from Baghdad.

The bishop was able to mistake Genghis Khan for a Christian king because Europe had long heard tantalizing rumors of a Christian potentate named Prester John who dwelt in the misty reaches of Asia. (In fact there *were* Christians in Asia—members of the Nestorian sect, which denied Christ's divinity and maintained that he was a holy, but mortal, prophet.) From time to time letters circulated throughout Europe describing the miraculous power of Prester John and his intention of launching a crusade against Islam. The letters were merely the work of imaginative forgers, but their fantasies were widely believed.

Above far left, coins minted by the Mongols in Persia. In 1294 the Mongol khan in Persia attempted to introduce paper money in an effort to replenish his government's exhausted treasury. Merchants refused to accept the notes, markets closed, riots broke out, and the government was forced to return to coinage. Below far left, a medallion struck in China during the Yüan period. The medallion, which was probably issued to a foreign trader, forbids the bearer to leave town.

Near left, a fourteenth-century Chinese painting depicting horses at a manger. Below, a thirteenth-century Mongol sword hilt.

39

Thus, when an army appeared out of the depths of mysterious Asia, it was assumed that the forces were led by one of the descendants of Prester John. European Jewry was also enthralled by the story of King David because one copy of the bishop's letter said that David was the king of Israel. The Jews immediately sent a shipment of gold to the Messiah, but the valuable treasure fell instead into the hands of Caucasian bandits.

Europe's hopes for a march on Jerusalem were dealt a blow when the pope received a disturbing letter from Queen Rusudan of Georgia, a kingdom in the Caucasus Mountains between the Black and Caspian seas. "A savage people of Tartars, hellish of aspect, as voracious as wolves in their hunger for spoils and as brave as lions, have invaded my country. . . . The brave knighthood of Georgia has hunted them out of the country, killing twenty-five thousand of the invaders." The invaders whom Rusudan called Tartars—a pun on the ethnic designation "Tatars" and the Latin word for "hell," *tartarus*—were actually a reconnaissance force of twenty thousand Mongols led by Jebe and Subotai. They had been dispatched by Genghis Khan, who was as ignorant of Europe as Europeans were of Mongolia, to find out what lands lay beyond the Caspian Sea. In 1221 and 1222 the Mongols defeated two Georgian armies, crossed the Caucasus in the middle of winter, and debouched into the steppes of southern Russia, where a tribe of nomads was waiting to repel them.

The army that met the Mongols comprised Cumans from the southern steppes under the leader-

Left, Kublai Khan's troops crossing the Yangtze River on a makeshift bridge of boats to besiege a city during the war against the Sung emperor of South China. Above, a Chinese artist's rendition of a Mongol hunter. Below, representatives of subject peoples bearing tribute to the court of the Yüan emperor. China's Yüan dynasty of Mongol emperors was founded by Kublai Khan in 1279, after the last Sung emperor was drowned as he fled from Mongol pursuers.

ship of Kotian, their king; Bulgars, who dwelt along the Volga; and other nomadic tribes. Exhausted by their arduous trek across the mountains, the Mongols resorted to trickery to divide their enemy. By night a delegation approached one of the Cuman camps with horses and gold to offer as tribute. The Cumans accepted the bribe and decamped, leaving Kotian and his allies to be defeated. The reconnaissance then began in earnest. Jebe rode west toward the Don River while Subotai scouted the coast of the Sea of Azov. Chancing upon a group of Venetian traders, Subotai obtained information about Russia and Europe in exchange for a treaty guaranteeing the safety of Venetian trading outposts. In the Mongol train were Moslem and Chinese surveyors and officials, who mapped the terrain, made estimates of crop production and the size of herds, and established a network of spies financed by Khwarizmian gold.

In the winter of 1222, Jebe and Subotai joined forces at the Dniester River, where they received reports of a confederation of Russians and Cumans, brought together by Kotian, rushing to expel the invading Mongols. In the thirteenth century, Russia was divided into contentious princedoms, unwilling to act together even in the face of a common danger. Kotian managed to persuade the Russian princes to form a coalition by offering gifts of camels, horses, and slave girls. The most enthusiastic of the Russians was Prince Mstislav the Daring of Galicia, who in the spring of 1223 persuaded several other princes to rendezvous with him on an island in the Dnieper River and then drive east. As they were on their way to the

river, the princes of Kiev and Chernigov were astonished to see Mongol ambassadors appear in their camp with a peace offering. The princes interpreted the offering as a sign of weakness and executed the delegates. Soon another ambassador arrived to accept their action as a declaration of war.

In the engagement that ensued, the generalship of the Russian princes proved to be considerably more limited than their confidence. The princes played right into the trap that Subotai set for them. Subotai stationed a rear guard of one thousand men on the east bank of the Dnieper opposite the Russian rallying point and withdrew east with his main force. The Russians eagerly fell upon this tiny contingent which fought to the last man, and then rushed chaotically after the retreating Subotai. For nine days the Mongols withdrew along the north coast of the Sea of Azov until they reached the river Kalka—where they had carefully chosen their ground. Without waiting for the arrival of their entire force, the pursuing Russians and Cumans attacked the Mongols. As the Mongol light cavalry poured arrow fire into the center of the onrushing enemy, the Cumans broke and fled, creating a gap that the Mongol heavy cavalry exploited. The Russian force retreated, colliding with their own reinforcements. The Mongols never broke formation and easily cut down forty thousand Russians.

The Mongols pursued the remnants of the Russian force all the way back to the Dnieper, some one hundred and fifty miles, where ten thousand Kievans were holding a hastily constructed fortress. Subotai called for a parley, and while the Kievans were off guard he stormed the fort. The prince of Kiev, who had touched off the conflict by slaying the Mongol ambassadors, was captured and put into a sealed box with two other nobles, where they slowly suffocated while Subotai, Jebe, and the other Mongol leaders enjoyed a victory banquet. The Mongols deemed this an honorable death for a prince because it was bloodless.

The Mongol expeditionary force, joined by reinforcements, rode north to subdue the Bulgars and then southeast to the Urals, where they defeated another nomad army of Kanglis. In the spring of 1223, Subotai returned to the khan's camp on the Irtish River; his companion Jebe died of a fever on the journey home.

Jebe was not the only general Genghis Khan lost that year. In China, the general Mukali died during the siege of a Chin city. Mukali had been placed in command of the Chin war when Genghis Khan was drawn away to fight the Kara-Khitan and the Khwarizmian shah. He prosecuted the war ruthlessly,

Facing page, a Chinese scroll of the thirteenth or fourteenth century, depicting various stages of a Mongol hunt. Using the same formations they took in battle, the Mongols formed an enormous circle around a region and then spent several weeks methodically closing the ring, allowing no animal to escape. When the prey was hemmed into a small space, the khan made the first kills with bow and arrow or trained falcons (above). His nobles then demonstrated their courage and skill by taking on the most ferocious animals, sometimes with their bare hands. At the end of one day's hunt, the animals not killed were permitted to escape and were protected by law from being poached until the next royal hunt.

but the forces of the Chin emperor stubbornly held out.

Genghis Khan was not fated to see the final victory of his armies in China. In 1226 the khan set out on a campaign against the Tanguts in Hsi Hsia, to the west of North China, and was severely injured in a fall from his horse. Though his generals urged him to put off the Tangut campaign, the khan refused, still enraged over an affront committed six years before. (The Tanguts, who had submitted to Genghis Khan just before he embarked on the Chinese war, gained a measure of independence under the khan by their timely surrender. But when Genghis Khan was gathering his armies for the Khwarizmian campaign and

The Mongol march of conquest

In less than a century the Mongols created the largest empire in world history, subjugating all of present-day Mongolia, China, Korea, Afghanistan, and Iran and parts of what are now Burma, Pakistan, Iraq, and the Soviet Union. All this was accomplished between 1211, when Genghis Khan began his invasion of China, and 1287, when Kublai Khan, Genghis Khan's grandson, conquered Burma.

China was a divided country at the time of Genghis Khan. The native Sung dynasty ruled only in South China, since North China was in the hands of the Chin—nomadic tribesmen who were regarded by the Chinese as barbarians. For this reason, the powerful Sung armies did not intervene when Genghis Khan launched his assault against the Chin in 1211. It nonetheless took the Mongols two years to penetrate the Great Wall that protected North China and another three years before Peking, the Chin capital, surrendered. Even the fall of Peking did not bring an end to the war; altogether, nearly two decades of bitter siege warfare were needed to wipe out Chin resistance.

In the Middle East the empire of the Seljuk Turks had disintegrated before the rise of Genghis Khan. Out of the eastern portion of the former Seljuk realm the shah of Khwarizm created a mighty state—one so rich and powerful that the shah felt confident enough to provoke a war with the Mongols in 1218. The shah was outwitted, though, in a lightning campaign staged by the brilliant Mongol strategist Subotai. With his armies in disarray but not yet decisively defeated, the shah fled west and was ultimately tracked down by a flying corps of Mongol horsemen. Jalal ad-Din, the son of the shah, rallied his father's scattered armies in western Khwarizm, but the Mongols' ruthless scorched-earth policy in the east made successful resistance impossible.

At the time of Genghis Khan's death in

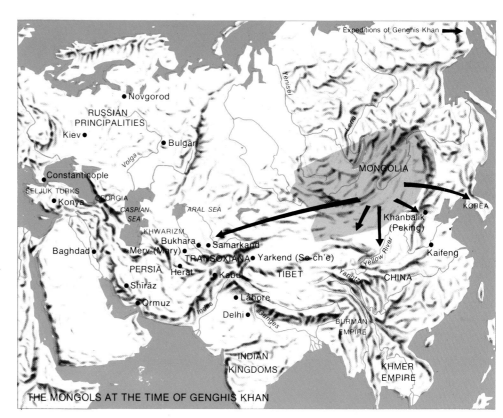

THE MONGOLS AT THE TIME OF GENGHIS KHAN

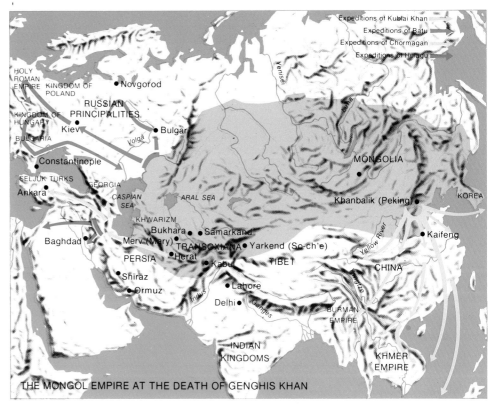

THE MONGOL EMPIRE AT THE DEATH OF GENGHIS KHAN

1227, undefeated Mongol armies had a strangle hold on central Asia. Western Asia and Europe lay open to attack. In 1235 the second great phase of Mongol conquest began under Genghis Khan's son and successor, Ogadai.

The new khan dispatched the general Chormagan to destroy the forces of Jalal ad-Din in 1236 and the following year launched an epic campaign in Russia and Europe. The leader of the expedition was

Ogadai's nephew Batu, and the field commander and chief strategist was the veteran general Subotai. In Russia the Mongols met with no concerted opposition. They spread terror through all the Russian lands except those in the northwest; that area was spared when a thaw turned the approaches to the stronghold of Novgorod into an uncrossable swamp. The prince of Novgorod, Alexander Nevski, later offered submission to the Mongols and won some

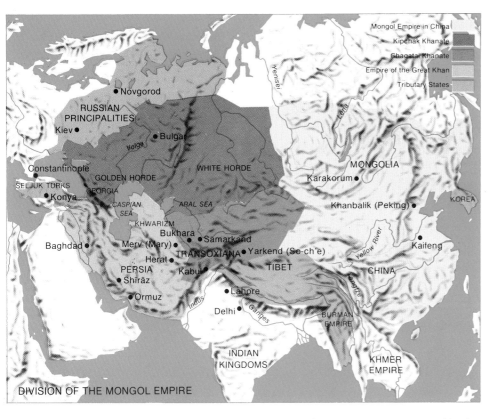

DIVISION OF THE MONGOL EMPIRE

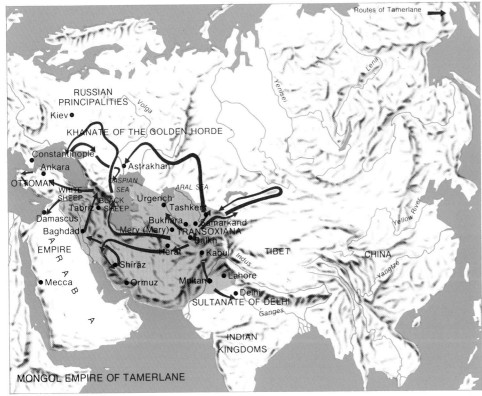

MONGOL EMPIRE OF TAMERLANE

by Ogadai's nephew Mangu. After his election in 1251, Mangu ordered the conquest of western Asia and the Sung empire in South China. His brother Hulagu undertook the western campaign, destroying the mountain castles of the Assassins (a secret order of Moslem fanatics) in 1257 and sacking Baghdad the following year. Another of Mangu's brothers, Kublai, was placed in charge of the Sung war. While with the Mongol armies in China in 1259, Mangu died. His death forced Hulagu to suspend fighting, and the small rear guard Hulagu left behind was defeated by Mameluke forces from Egypt, ending the Mongol conquest of western Asia.

Civil war broke out in the Mongol Empire after the death of Mangu, with Kublai and his brother Arik-Boko vying for power. Both had been elected great khan—Kublai in China and Arik-Boko at the Mongol capital of Karakorum. After Kublai's army defeated his brother's forces, Kublai was accepted as khan throughout the empire.

Kublai divided the Mongol realm into four khanates. He personally retained control of China, declaring a new dynasty—the Yüan. The khanate in central Asia was placed under the rule of the descendants of Genghis Khan's second son, Jagatai. The Golden Horde and the White Horde were set over the Kipchak khanate, named for a nomadic tribe the Mongols had displaced in southern Russia. Hulagu was given the Il-Khanate in western Asia.

Kublai completed the conquest of South China in 1279, but his ambition led him to invade Japan and Java; both ventures ended unsuccessfully. Kublai's forces, though victorious in Burma, were turned back by Khmer defenders in Southeast Asia.

The Mongol Empire proved to be short-lived. The Chinese expelled their detested overlords about seventy-five years after the death of Kublai Khan in 1294. The Russian princes grew restive under the Mongol khans of the Golden Horde and finally gained their independence in the late fifteenth century. Factional disputes crippled Mongol control of the Il-Khanate, creating a political vacuum in the fourteenth century that was filled by Tamerlane, a descendant of Genghis Khan. Tamerlane warred on the Golden Horde, conquered much of western Asia, and invaded India, but the empire disintegrated after his death in 1405.

freedom for his realm, which was never occupied by the Mongol army.

After destroying Kiev in 1240, the army of Batu and Subotai headed west, defeating the knights of eastern Europe at Liegnitz and Mohi in 1241. These victories opened the gates of central Europe to the Mongols. Mongol forces were poised to invade Austria when news reached Batu, early in 1242, that Ogadai had died at the end of the preceding year. Batu immediately withdrew his armies to southern Russia to await the election of a new khan; there he set up a capital at Sarai, from which Mongol khans were to rule Russia for the next two centuries. Batu's army became known as the Golden Horde; dissension among the Mongol princes later split the horde in two, with a White Horde forming in the east.

Ogadai's eldest son, Kuyuk, reigned for only two years as khan; he was succeeded

The fabulous trek of Marco Polo

Six and a half centuries after his death, Marco Polo is still a legendary figure—the archetype of the traveler who visits previously unknown lands of mystery and splendor and lives to tell the tale. Marco arrived at the Peking court of Kublai Khan in 1275 with his father and uncle. The khan was impressed with twenty-year-old Marco, gave him a post in the government, and ordered him to roam throughout China as the emperor's observer. For seventeen years, Marco lived in China, which had previously been seen by only a handful of Europeans.

Just before their patron's death, the Polos were able to make their way back to Italy. According to legend they arrived in rags and were turned away from their own house. After persuading skeptical relatives that they were indeed the long-lost Polos, the travelers cut open their tattered cloaks—and jewels cascaded to the floor. Marco later wrote his *Description of the World,* which revealed to Europeans for the first time such wonders as asbestos, coal, and paper money. His vivid accounts of the people and customs of Asia amazed Europe and helped bring about the age of explorers seeking land and water routes to the fabulous realm of Kublai Khan.

Below, Niccolò and Maffeo Polo, Marco Polo's father and uncle, leaving Constantinople on their first journey to the East. On arrival in China, the Polos were invited to the court of Kublai Khan, who was always eager to meet foreigners. Near right, the arrival of the Polos—with Marco in their company—at the Persian port of Hormuz during the second trip to China.

Above, a section of Fra Mauro's world map of 1459, one of the most important maps of the century. Fra Mauro's delineation of Asia was based entirely on Marco Polo's accounts. The section shown above depicts Peking, then known as Cambaluc or Khanbalik—the "khan's city." The word "Chataio" on the map indicates Cathay (China).

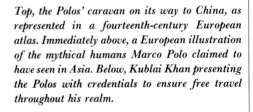

Top, the Polos' caravan on its way to China, as represented in a fourteenth-century European atlas. Immediately above, a European illustration of the mythical humans Marco Polo claimed to have seen in Asia. Below, Kublai Khan presenting the Polos with credentials to ensure free travel throughout his realm.

requested troops from Hsi Hsia, the Tanguts sent an insulting reply to the effect that if the khan didn't already have enough men he shouldn't presume to rule an empire.) The war of revenge dragged on for over a year, and its hardships fatally weakened the great Genghis Khan. He died on August 24, 1227.

News of the khan's death was kept secret to avoid the possibility of revolt in the empire; the cortege that carried Genghis Khan's body back to his homeland moved in silence, and every person who inadvertently met the procession was killed. After more than three months of mourning, the Mongols buried Genghis Khan at a site he had selected himself—on the mountain of Burkan-Kaldun, where he had hunted all his life. After the burial the grave was never visited again by the Mongols, and its location is unknown today.

For his vast achievements, Genghis Khan is counted as one of history's greatest figures. In four decades he created a nation out of wandering tribesmen; built a skilled, disciplined army and placed it in the hands of brilliant commanders; and laid the foundations of an administrative structure and a legal system. Though his people esteemed him as a just ruler, Genghis Khan can hardly be considered an enlightened or civilized monarch. He advanced no ideal or program, destroyed what he could not immediately use, and contemplated the enslavement of entire nations in a medieval version of a "new order"—one that his successors nearly made a reality.

The empire lost none of its vigor despite the death of its founder: Genghis Khan's laws were still strictly obeyed, his policy of religious tolerance and system of administration were maintained, and the armies remained disciplined and loyal. Before his death, Genghis Khan had divided the empire among his sons and their descendants, who were to be under the sovereignty of the new great khan soon to be elected. Jagatai was given the lands of the old Khwarizmian Empire and the regions east of them to the Altai Mountains; Ogadai was made ruler of China; Tului received the traditional legacy of the youngest son— the homeland; and the sons of Genghis Khan's de-

Though the Mongols themselves were not proficient artists, they allowed the arts to flourish in the lands they ruled. The Yüan (Mongol) period in China witnessed the high point of the Chinese theater—a product of frustrated Confucian scholars turned literati. Among the sculptures dating from the Yüan era are this wooden carving of a Buddhist disciple (left) and this terra-cotta statuette of a whistling actor (right).

49

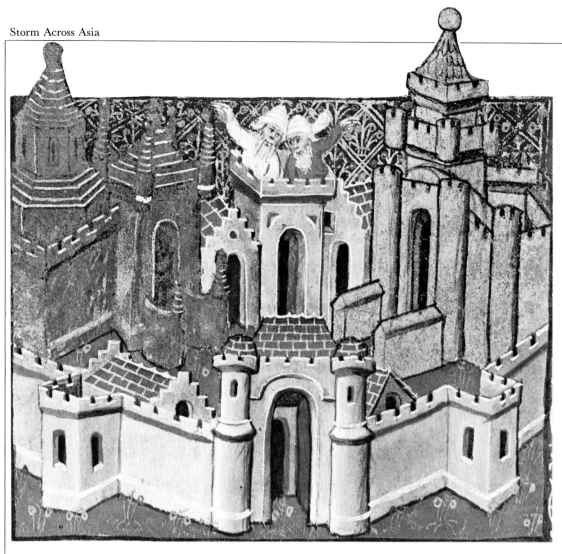

These pages, illustrations of Asian cities visited by Marco Polo, from a French work that dates to about the turn of the fifteenth century. Left, a Persian city that the French artist took to be covered with silver and gold, though the decorations were probably mosaics.

These pages, illustrations of Asian cities visited by Marco Polo, from a French work that dates to about the turn of the fifteenth century. Left, a Persian city that the French artist took to be covered with silver and gold, though the decorations were probably mosaics.

Europe's view of Asia's cities

Right, a view of the city called Comady by Marco Polo. Above far right, a city in Bactria (present-day Afghanistan).

Below, the city of Hangchow, where Marco Polo served as Kublai Khan's governor. In Marco's enthusiastic description, the city was one hundred miles in circumference and had twelve thousand stone bridges.

The cities Marco Polo saw in Asia were more wealthy, populous, and splendid than any in Europe. Multistoried buildings, impressive earthworks and canals, and colorful mosaic decorations astounded the young Venetian. Even the statistics of food consumption were mind-boggling—ninety tons of rice and five tons of pepper per day in the case of one Chinese city. Flourishing trade led to the emergence of a class of merchants who flaunted their wealth.

Private affluence could not compare with the fabulous riches of the khan. Marco found the walls of the khan's palace "covered in gold and silver," and during Marco's stay the khan was engaged in building a new city at Peking. Marco's breathless descriptions of the great cities of China and Persia amazed Europe, whose artists took up the challenge of illustrating his account with the vignettes depicted on these pages.

On his way to Tibet, Marco Polo stopped at the city of Sindafa, currently called Chengtu, in Szechwan. Below left, a view of a bridge in Sindafa, showing a boat being pulled in by a man and a mule. Immediately below, another view of the city. The design of the boat and the city's architecture are actually European.

City life in Mongol China

Marco Polo's account of his seventeen years in China includes lively descriptions of the common people, their customs, and their way of life in the cities. The Italian traveler was struck by the bustle of the cit-

These pages, illustrations from Street Scenes During Peacetime, *a collection of miniatures by the Chinese artist Chu Yün Ming. The men and women in the scene at center have probably gathered to watch some kind of street performance. Below, two men restraining an antagonist in a fight. Below right, a donkey carrying a load of wood.*

ies and the wealth of many of the inhabitants. "On every market day the squares were crowded with tradespeople, who cover the whole space with the articles brought by carts and boats. . . . The men as well as the women have fair complexions, and are handsome. The greater part of them are always clothed in silk." So successful were the owners of workshops, according to Marco Polo, that they did not have to work, and their wives did nothing but indulge their "delicate and languid habits." The wealthy spent much of their time promenading along city streets or taking carriages to lush parks, where they could retire to "shady recesses contrived by gardeners."

During the Mongol period, the streets of Chinese cities emptied at night—by order of the Mongol governors, who feared "tumult or insurrection." A curfew was strictly enforced and cities were blacked out. These measures effectively controlled the large city populations, which grew increasingly restive under Mongol rule.

Above left, two workmen carrying sticks and ropes. Above right, a street entertainer with a monkey trained to perform tricks.

Above, a village carved out of hillside rock in Persia. Below, a domed tomb and minaret in Khorasan, a province of Persia that suffered terrible devastation in Genghis Khan's war on Khwarizm.

Above, a portrait of Hulagu, a grandson of Genghis Khan who was placed in charge of the conquest of western Asia by his brother Mangu Khan. Hulagu succeeded in conquering Persia and parts of Syria—the area that constituted the Il-Khanate and became autonomous after Kublai Khan's death.

ceased eldest son, Juji, were given an open-ended legacy—the land to the north and west to the Altai, as far as Mongol arms could conquer.

In accordance with Genghis Khan's wishes, the Mongol princes elected Ogadai as great khan in 1229. Ogadai first turned his attention to the conquest of China. After the hard-pressed Chin emperor committed suicide in 1234, however, Ogadai set aside the subjugation of the Sung Empire of South China in favor of a more distant undertaking—the conquest of the lands Genghis Khan had promised the heirs of Juji. Juji's son Batu was placed in command of the venture. He was to be accompanied by numerous

Mongol princes and by the old general Subotai, who would serve as the military mastermind of the operation. In 1236 a horde of one hundred fifty thousand Mongols and Turks set out on a campaign that would last seven years and nearly destroy the political structure of Europe.

The Mongols' first objective was to secure the region between the Volga River and the Urals by subduing the Bulgars and the eastern branch of the Cumans, called the Kipchaks. The Bulgar capital, at the confluence of the Volga and Kama rivers, was taken, and in the regions north of the Caspian the Kipchak people were routed and their king slain. A

This citadel (left) near Lake Van in eastern Turkey was one of the strongholds of the Armenian kingdom of King Hayton, who wisely allied his small realm with the Mongol Empire and thus saved Armenia from Mongol devastation. Below, Hulagu's siege of Baghdad, the seat of the leader of Islam—the caliph. This illustration shows a bridge of boats over the Tigris River, which the Mongols diverted to flood the plain around Baghdad and cut off the defenders.

large number of these subdued nomads were conscripted into the Mongol army, but Batu also sold some Kipchak warriors into slavery in Egypt—a move that later Mongol leaders would regret. The Egyptian descendants of the Kipchaks rose to power as the Mamelukes, who were to contest Mongol control in western Asia in the mid-thirteenth century.

After their western flank was secured, the Mongols moved into Russia. Subotai chose to begin the invasion in the province of Ryazan, the weakest point on the Russian frontier. The province was ruled by no fewer than four princes who were under the control of Grand Prince Yuri of Vladimir, a princedom to the

north. The town of Ryazan was stormed and sacked, and a relief party sent by the grand prince was intercepted and slaughtered. After taking Moscow, then just a small but strategically important town, the Mongol army divided into two parts: Subotai headed north to face whatever force Yuri would send against him, and Batu marched on Novgorod. The grand prince marshaled his armies and dispatched a reconnaissance party that returned with the laconic report: "My lord, the Tatars have surrounded us." Subotai fell upon the hapless grand prince's army and annihilated it.

Batu was having less luck on the road to Novgorod.

Because he delayed two weeks to besiege a small town, by the time Batu neared Novgorod the spring thaw had turned the approaches into swamps. Never ones to fight on unfavorable ground, the Mongols withdrew south for the summer. Fresh supplies and horses arrived from Mongolia, and the surrounding tribes were plundered for food. The success of the winter campaign inflated the pride of the Mongol princes and led to a break between Batu and Kuyuk, Ogadai's son. The two engaged in a petty argument over who should take the first drink at a banquet—a matter of honor among the princes—and Kuyuk stormed out of the camp. Kuyuk returned to the cap-

Preceding pages, a Persian miniature of the siege of Baghdad in 1258. After Hulagu's engineers diverted the Tigris River to flood the plain around the city, the Mongols set about leveling the walls with the siege engines seen in the foreground. Above, a coin with the image of Abaka, Hulagu's son and successor as Il-Khan. Top, a feast scene with Arghun, the son of Abaka, seated alongside one of his wives. Right, a view of Aleppo, a town in Syria captured by Hulagu in 1260.

ital Ogadai had established at Karakorum, where he found his father in a rage. Ogadai rebuked Kuyuk for quarreling with his commander and sent him back to Batu with orders to put aside his own feelings for the good of the army.

The last objective in the Russian campaign was the once-flourishing city of Kiev, more than five centuries old. Kiev had grown prosperous from trade and boasted thirty gold-domed churches, but its recent decline deprived Russia of a centralized defense against the Mongols. The Mongols besieged the town, knocked apart a wooden gate with artillery, and stormed in. The terrified garrison fought val-iantly, but the city was taken amid great slaughter, and all its churches save one were razed.

The destruction of Kiev in December 1240 ended all major Russian resistance to the Mongol invasion. Novgorod and the rest of northeastern Russia escaped destruction when Prince Alexander Nevski of Novgorod offered to submit to the Mongol rule. Prince Alexander initiated a policy of peaceful cooperation with the Mongol overlords that the other principalities reluctantly went along with—though some nobles attempted, without success, to persuade the pope to dispatch an army against the pagan invaders.

With the conquest of Russia complete, Subotai

Above, the mosque of the Ommiads at Damascus. The city, which fell to Hulagu's forces in 1260 without a fight, was later in the year captured by the Mamelukes of Egypt, who wrested Syria from the Mongols. Above right, a gold coin from the reign of the Il-Khan Ghazan (1295–1304), an enlightened and energetic ruler. Right, the lavish field tent of Ghazan.

An empire won on horseback

The Mongol empire was borne from its home on the Asian steppe to the shores of the Pacific and the Adriatic on horseback. The Mongol army was entirely cavalry, and conquered territories could be efficiently administered because the khans were able to communicate quickly with their subjects by mounted couriers.

. Both rider and horse were inured to hardship: A Mongol learned to sleep in the saddle as his horse continued on a forced march. On a long journey without water, a Mongol would slit open one of his mount's veins, drink the blood, and bandage the wound before pressing on. In winter the horses foraged by scraping the snow to get at grass.

Mounts that had served in battle were never killed for food, even if they were injured. So close was the tie between man and animal that a Mongol's horse was often buried with him. Not surprisingly, horses were a preferred subject in art for the Mongols–Chinese artists dependent on Mongol patronage found that their masters wanted little else.

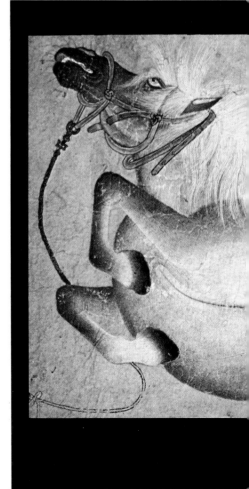

Top, a thirteenth-century silver medallion depicting a Mongol soldier on horseback. Immediately above, a Chinese painting depicting Mongols with a horse, accurately rendered as a stocky, short-legged creature. Right, a set of iron stirrups that Genghis Khan gave to his grandson Hulagu.

A number of miniature paintings by Mehmet Siah-i-Qalam, a Turkish artist of the fourteenth and fifteenth centuries, depict the life of the nomad. Left, a nomad and his horse on the silk route. Below left, a nomad training a horse to take a rider.

Top, a thirteenth-century Persian depiction of a Mongol horseman. Immediately above, a Mongol rider in a Chinese painting of the Ming dynasty.

mapped a brilliant campaign—in plan similar to the Khwarizmian war—that was destined to take the Mongol army to the Adriatic Sea. Strengthened by tens of thousands of prisoners, some of whom were conscripted into the army, a Mongol force of some hundred thousand men headed west. Their chief objective was the kingdom of Hungary, ruled by King Béla IV, who had one of the most powerful armies in Europe at his command. Béla also had the help of Kotian and the tens of thousands of Cumans who had fled into Hungary after their defeat by the Mongols.

Subotai divided his forces for the assault on Hungary, sending a detachment north into Poland and Lithuania to prevent their princes from sending aid to Béla. The Polish princes heard of the invasion too late to prepare a defense; the inhabitants of Kraków received just enough warning to flee before the Mongol troops arrived and burned the town. The Mongols pressed on, and at Liegnitz, they annihilated a hastily gathered Polish force that included a detachment of Teutonic Knights. After the battle, according to a Polish historian, the Mongols severed an ear from each corpse and sent the grisly tokens to Batu in nine sacks.

King Béla knew that his situation was desperate. Although determined to fight, he received more hindrance than help from his vassals and supposed allies. Hungary was a feudal state, and Béla was dependent on the support of his barons, who mistrusted the Cumans and feared that Béla was using the Mongol threat as a means to consolidate his position. When the barons stubbornly refused to march under Béla's command, the king appealed to the pope and the Holy Roman emperor, but his pleas were ignored. Frederick, the duke of Austria, did come with soldiers—ostensibly to help Béla but actually to further his own ends by exacerbating Béla's troubles with his barons. After a brief visit, during which he supported the barons in their refusal to unite with Béla, Frederick and his troops withdrew.

To gain time for negotiating with his barons, Béla fortified the passes through the Carpathians. Batu and Subotai, however, overwhelmed these outposts and rushed toward the Danube, where an army of a hundred thousand Hungarians under Béla's direct command was waiting at the twin cities of Buda and Pest. Even then the barons refused to fight, and in their insane malice they treacherously assassinated Kotian. The enraged Cumans abandoned King Béla and made their way to Bulgaria, looting as they went.

Toward the end of March 1241, Subotai and Batu, drawn up at the gates of Pest, signaled their army in Poland to join them. Before any attempt had been made to dislodge the Mongols, Subotai and Batu

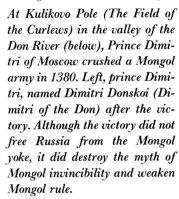

At Kulikovo Pole (The Field of the Curlews) in the valley of the Don River (below), Prince Dimitri of Moscow crushed a Mongol army in 1380. Left, prince Dimitri, named Dimitri Donskoi (Dimitri of the Don) after the victory. Although the victory did not free Russia from the Mongol yoke, it did destroy the myth of Mongol invincibility and weaken Mongol rule.

Russia finally attained its independence in 1480, one hundred years after the battle at Kulikovo Pole, when Prince Ivan III of Moscow refused to pay obeisance to the Mongol khan. Russia was then able to begin rebuilding its ravaged cities. Far left, the cathedral of Santa Sophia in Kiev, the only building that survived the Mongol siege of 1240. Near left, the Church of the Transfiguration, erected in Suzdal in the 1750s, when Russia was regaining a measure of its former glory.

Preceding pages, an illustration from a Hungarian chronicle depicting the arrival of the Cuman tribe in Hungary. The Cumans lived in the steppes of southern Russia until driven out by the Mongol invasion in 1236. The Cumans and their king, Kotian, were welcomed into Hungary by King Béla, who needed allies in the coming war against the Mongols. The Hungarian nobles, however, mistrusted the Cumans and killed Kotian, bringing an end to the short-lived alliance just a few days before the Mongols annihilated a Hungarian army at Mohi.

Right, a portrait of Tamerlane. In his seventy-year lifetime, Tamerlane forged an empire out of the shambles of the Mongol realm; his successors, though, were unable to hold these territories together. Left, a Persian miniature depicting the birth of Tamerlane in 1336 near Samarkand.

suddenly retreated. The astounded barons eagerly joined Béla and his hundred thousand troops in what they thought would be a playful pursuit ending in the mass slaughter of the Mongols. In reality, Subotai was choosing his ground for a single, decisive battle. The Mongols retreated east across the Sajó River by means of a stone bridge near a heath called Mohi and waited for the Hungarians to arrive on the opposite bank. The site that the Hungarians would occupy was boxed in by rivers, hills, and thickets: Once in place an army would be trapped.

Under cover of night, Subotai moved south with thirty thousand Mongols and a detachment of engineers, who threw a pontoon bridge across the Sajó. In the morning, when the Hungarians formed their battle line, Batu ordered a barrage of fire bombs, which confused the Hungarian cavalry and forced it to give ground. Protected by his artillery fire, Batu crossed the stone bridge and engaged Béla's troops. Subotai's attack on the Hungarian rear was late—he had been delayed crossing the river—so Batu's men were at first

hard pressed. But when Subotai appeared, the Hungarians were surrounded and pelted from all sides with arrows. Batu commanded another artillery barrage and tightened the ring around the Hungarians. When the Hungarians tried to break out they were cut down. Sixty thousand Hungarians died in the battle at Mohi, though Béla himself escaped.

After consolidating his hold over eastern Hungary in the summer and autumn of 1241, Batu crossed the frozen Danube on Christmas Day, stormed the wealthy city of Gran, and sent a detachment of riders to pursue the fugitive king Béla to a fortress on the Adriatic. This small party, unable to attack Béla's fort, was galloping south toward Dubrovnik, and the main army was preparing to invade Austria—without any substantial opposition—when messengers reached Batu with word that Ogadai had died. Batu immediately broke off the campaign and turned east.

Had the campaign continued, it is probable that Batu's army, which was never defeated by Europe's knights, could have swept all the way to the Atlantic:

The pope and the Holy Roman emperor were political enemies who would never have fielded a combined army against Batu. Further, it is unlikely that in all of Europe could a general have been found to match the strategic genius Subotai. As the Mongols marched inexorably across Hungary, Europe's royalty adopted a fatalistic attitude. In a letter, the French king wrote philosophically that he was prepared to die at the hands of the Mongols and "enter Heaven to enjoy the rapture that awaits the elect."

Mongol law required that all Genghis Khan's descendants be present for the election of a new khan.

Because his enemy Kuyuk was the favored choice, Batu delayed the election for a period of five years by refusing to go to Karakorum. At length, his patience exhausted and his temper seething, Kuyuk peremptorily summoned Batu, but the latter excused himself from attending on the dubious grounds that he had a sore foot.

A description of Kuyuk's election has survived in an account by Giovanni de Piano Carpini, an Italian priest dispatched as an emissary by Pope Innocent IV to chastise the Mongols for their bloody assault on Europe and to propose conversion to Christianity. Despite his sixty years, Carpini was eager to visit the

Left, a portrait of Tamerlane and his sons. At his death in 1405, Tamerlane's empire stretched from the Indus River to the Black Sea and from the Persian Gulf to the Aral Sea. Tamerlane divided his realm among his sons and grandsons, who warred among themselves for four years before a successor emerged.

Right, a feast in Tamerlane's court at Samarkand. Though the conqueror spent little time in his capital city, he built magnificent palaces and summoned scholars, artists, and artisans from all over his dominions to enrich the city's cultural life. Below, a duck sculpted in metal—an example of Persian art from the period of Tamerlane's reign.

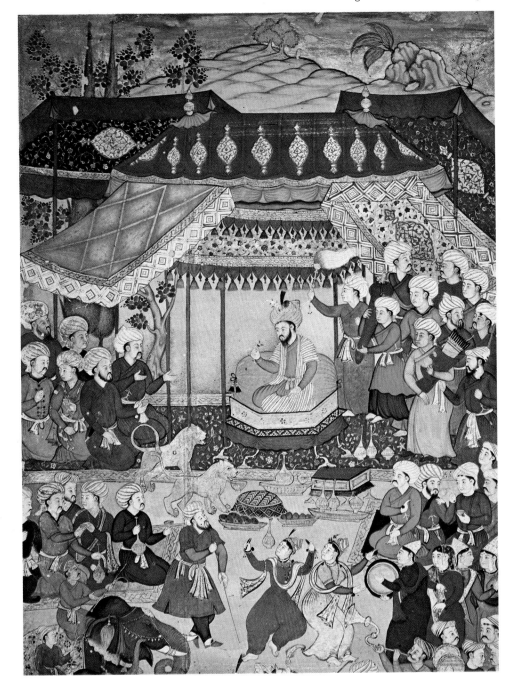

distant lands of the mysterious invaders and set off from Lyon, France, on Easter Sunday in 1245. He reached Mongolia in July of the following year, when preparations were under way for the election of the khan. The priest was lodged in a camp outside Karakorum, where ambassadors had gathered from all the subject nations of the empire to pay homage to the new leader. Kuyuk was elected amid merry feasting and lavish gift giving—a source of acute embarrassment to Carpini, since he himself had no tribute offering to make. (In the account of his journey, the priest reported seeing five hundred wagons heaped with gold, silver, jewels, and silks—all offered to win the favor of Kuyuk.) The new khan was naturally disgruntled to hear that the pope's emissary had arrived empty-handed. So great was his pique that he cut off Carpini's food supply; the priest survived only

69

Right, a view of the Bolan Pass in Pakistan, through which Tamerlane's army traveled on its invasion of India in 1398. Below, a depiction of Tamerlane's army storming a city, from a fifteenth-century Persian history of Tamerlane's conquests.

Right and top left, Persian miniatures of the fifteenth century, depicting the dress and weapons of Tamerlane's forces. Above, the Bolan River in Baluchistan, a province of present-day Pakistan. The province was devastated by Genghis Khan's troops during the war against Khwarizm and later formed part of Tamerlane's empire. Bordered on the west by Iran and on the north by Afghanistan, Baluchistan is an arid, mountainous region inhabited today by nomads.

went on to order the pope to appear before him in submission and ended on a foreboding note: "If you do not observe God's command, I shall know you as my enemy."

Carpini was permitted to leave Mongolia in November 1246. He rejected an oblique suggestion that Mongol ambassadors accompany him back to Europe, fearing that the Mongols would be encouraged to initiate a fresh campaign of conquest after seeing the weak and divided condition of the

through the kind offices of a Russian goldsmith, who furnished him with provisions.

Kuyuk's vexation was further aggravated when Pope Innocent's letter of rebuke was read to him. The irritated khan dictated a contemptuous reply, contained in a document discovered in the Vatican archives in 1920. Referring to the pope's sharp statements on the Mongol slaughter of Europeans, Kuyuk said: "I do not understand these words of yours. The Eternal Heaven has slain and annihilated these peoples, because they have adhered neither to Genghis Khan nor to the Khagan [Kuyuk], both of whom have been sent to make known God's command." He

Below, a detail of a Turkish miniature depicting the battle of Shibukabad, fought between Tamerlane's army and the Ottoman Turks in 1402 near Ankara. Left, the Turkish sultan Bayezid I, known as the Thunderbolt, who defeated armies of Hungarians and Crusaders but failed to capture Constantinople after a six-year siege.

West. After another difficult trek across Asia, Carpini reached Kiev in June 1247. He reported Kuyuk's threats to Europe and painted a sobering picture of the wealth and power of the Mongols, whose intention, he claimed, was "to overthrow the whole world and reduce it to slavery."

Kuyuk did not live to carry out any of his threats against Europe and the pope. Two years after his selection as khan, while enroute to demand submission from the rebellious Batu, Kuyuk died. He was succeeded by Tului's son Mangu, whose election was marked by intrigue and followed by a ruthless purge of opponents. Under Mangu Khan, Batu's fief, known as the Golden Horde, became virtually independent of the rest of the empire.

The reign of Mangu Khan (1251–1259) was short but prosperous. Mangu made extensive improvements in the Mongol capital of Karakorum, located in the Mongol heartland south of Lake Baikal. Although the walled city of Mangu's time was only about one and a half square miles in size, settlements stretched out from it on all sides, and the city boasted

Buddhist and Taoist temples, Moslem mosques, and a Nestorian Christian church. Mangu had his palace designed in the Chinese style and commissioned thousands of craftsmen from all over the world, including a goldsmith from Paris.

The first European to describe Karakorum was a French missionary named William of Rubruck, whose serious-minded visit to the Mongols produced a rather humorous clash of cultures. William was a member of the order of the Franciscans, whose members customarily were clean-shaven and went barefoot; the Mongols took the absence of a beard as a sign of barbarity and regarded anyone who went un-

Above, Tamerlane, seated on a throne, receiving the defeated Bayezid I after the battle
of Shibukabad. Bayezid was captured after
the battle and imprisoned in a wire-mesh
cage; he died after a year of captivity.

Left, a battle between Tamerlane's forces and
Ottoman Turks, as depicted in a fourteenth-
century miniature. Tamerlane's victory over
Bayezid I in 1402 delayed the expansion of
the Turkish Empire only temporarily. The
weakness and disunity of Tamerlane's realm
after his death gave the Turks a free hand in
the Middle East; they pushed the Mamelukes
out of Egypt and eventually extended their
rule across North Africa and into Hungary,
founding an empire that lasted in part until
1918.

The beast in the desert

Though the Mongols were basically horse-men, they recognized the usefulness of the camel as a beast of burden in the vast tracts of their empire in Asia that were desert. The camel is admirably equipped by nature to live in the desert: It can stand extremes of heat and cold; its large feet prevent the animal from sinking into the sand; and in high winds its nostrils close up to keep out the blowing sand. The international caravan trade between Europe and Asia was entirely dependent on these patient beasts, which are able to travel great distances without nourishment. Short rests at the few oases along the caravan routes, during which the camels built up a store of fat in their humps for the next stage of the journey, were sufficient for the animals to refresh themselves. The camel's hump was the subject of a Mongol saying: "The camel calls the dromedary a hunchback"—the Mongol equivalent of the pot calling the kettle black.

Top, left to right, an autumn landscape at an oasis along the silk route in Afghanistan; a two-humped Bactrian camel; a detail of a miniature showing men unloading camels at a market; a Chinese painting of a caravan stopping for the night. Left, three camels, as depicted in a sixteenth-century Persian miniature. Below, a herd of camels in the Gobi Desert today.

Under a richly decorated tent (above), Tamerlane receives one of his sons, Omar Sheik, the governor of the recently conquered territories of Syria and Mesopotamia. This scene took place during Tamerlane's two-year campaign in India (1398-1399), launched in part to chastise the Indians for not spreading the Islamic faith and in part for plunder. Right, the Indus River, crossed by Tamerlane's army in 1398.

Tamerlane's conquests were marked by a savagery equaling that of Genghis Khan. After the conquest of Delhi in 1399, Tamerlane's army massacred the inhabitants (far right) and built a tower out of their skulls. In Russia, archaeologists excavating battlefields where Tamerlane fought the Golden Horde have found masses of skeletons with severed heads and limbs.

shodden in the cold climate of Mongolia as nothing short of insane. Mangu himself impressed his visitor as a handsome man, and the friar admired the khan's fine sealskin cloak—but William uncharitably described the khan's daughter as "very ugly." Once during William's stay at Karakorum, the khan, who was fond of theological disputation, arranged a debate for all the religious representatives at his court. William inconclusively argued the existence of God with the Buddhists as the khan and his court proceeded to get drunk.

The expansion of the Mongol Empire continued under Mangu, who dispatched his brother Kublai

and the veteran general Subotai to subdue the Sung emperors of South China. Another brother, Hulagu, was sent to enlarge the empire in the west by assaulting the Islamic nation of Syria and two independent powers that blocked the way: the Caliphate of Baghdad and the Ismaili Order of Assassins, a fanatical sect of political murderers. Hulagu first destroyed the Assassins' fortresses in the Elburz Mountains south of the Caspian and killed or captured most of the order's adherents. From the Elburz, Hulagu turned south to Baghdad, where his engineers demolished dams along the Tigris River and flooded the plain around the city. After the caliph and his sons were forced to sur-

render, Hulagu made them host a grotesque banquet in the ruins of the city; he then had the caliph sewn into a carpet and trampled to death by horses.

In 1259, when Hulagu was preparing to march on Jerusalem in an alliance with the Crusaders, Mangu Khan suddenly died of dysentery while fighting in China. Once again the death of a khan brought an end to a Mongol campaign on the brink of success. The following year a rear guard of twenty-five thousand Mongols left behind by Hulagu was annihilated by Mameluke forces from Egypt. The battle, which took place at Ain Jalut in Palestine, signaled the end of Mongol expansion in the west.

The death of Mangu also brought civil war to the Mongol Empire. In China, Mangu's brother Kublai was elected great khan, but another brother, Arik-Boko, asserted that the election was invalid because it had not been held in Karakorum. Behind this legalistic dispute was a deep ideological division: Arik-Boko led a faction of conservative Mongols intent on retaining the traditional nomadic way of life—extracting wealth from the empire without intermingling with the vanquished people or becoming entangled in complex governments. Kublai, however, realized that an empire won on horseback could not be governed on horseback and intended to establish a government in China with a permanent, urban structure. The

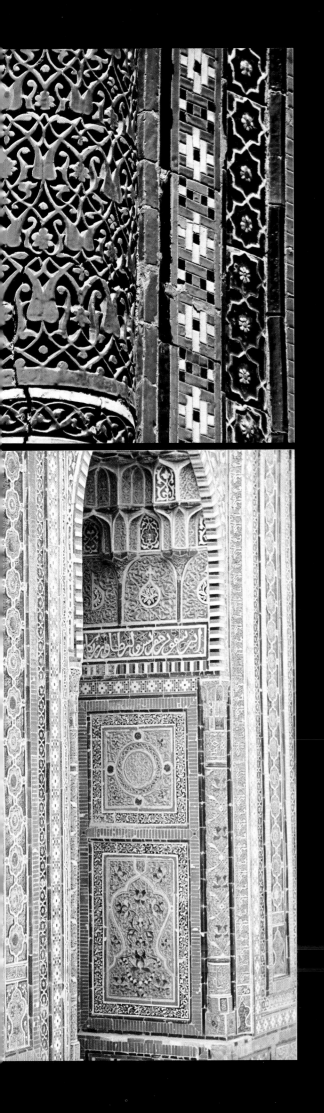

sophistication of the Chinese appealed to him—though he had no intention of abolishing or relaxing military discipline.

Kublai's generals defeated the supporters of Arik-Boko, and the timely deaths of Kublai's enemies in the Golden Horde ended opposition in the west. Kublai Khan was then able to complete the conquest of South China in 1279 and assume control of a wealthy but war-torn country. Kublai Khan set about to restore the country, building hospitals and poorhouses throughout China and feeding thirty thousand indigents in Peking every day from imperial kitchens. The canal system that brought food to the cities was expanded, and in years of good harvest the government bought the excess food to distribute free in times of famine. To promote trade throughout the empire and with Europe, Kublai Khan improved the system of imperial roads that linked China with Russia, establishing ten thousand depots—one every thirty or so miles—where travelers could get fresh horses or spend the night. In Siberia, trained dog teams pulled messengers, traders, and goods from one station to the next. Robbery was nonexistent because the entire system was patrolled by Mongol cavalry, leading one chronicler to boast that "a maiden bearing a nugget of gold on her head could wander safely through the realm."

In the atmosphere of this "Pax Mongolica" three travelers from Venice—Marco Polo, his father, and his uncle—arrived at Kublai Khan's court, where they were dazzled by scenes of incredible wealth. Ten thousand workmen were engaged in building a new city: "the great court" just north of Peking. Its fourteen square miles held a park with a menagerie, gardens filled with trees brought from all over Asia by elephant, ponds stocked with exotic fish, and an artificial hill covered with shrubs and ornamental rocks and surmounted by a pavilion. One tract of land had been planted with steppe grass to remind the khan of his Mongolian homeland. In the splendor of this nearly completed court, twenty-year-old Marco met the khan and impressed him with detailed descriptions of the journey to China. Because it was the

Preceding pages, the complex of mausoleums outside of Samarkand, where Tamerlane's skeleton was found by archaeologists in 1941. These pages, details of Samarkand's architectural splendors. Samarkand flourished under Tamerlane and his successors. The miniature at center shows the hanging of the architect of a Samarkand mosque, who was suspected of having an affair with a wife of Tamerlane.

81

The wives of the conquerors

The Mongols were polygamous, and the accepted means of selecting a bride was kidnaping (until Genghis Khan outlawed the custom). On the whole, however, women enjoyed a much higher status in Mongol society than in Arab and Persian cultures. Hunting and war were male concerns, but onerous household duties were divided between men and women. The women drove the wagons, milked the cows and mares, tanned hides, sewed, knitted, and made the felt coverings for the yurts. Men undertook repairs and carpentry work.

In matters of both peace and war, Mongol leaders sought the advice of their wives, who sometimes offered counsel that male advisers shied away from. Borte, one of Genghis Khan's wives, was the first to suggest that he set up his own camp apart from the other chiefs—a decision that contributed to his election as khan. Another of his wives prudently recommended that he choose a successor before setting out for the Khwarizmian war, whereas the khan's male counselors were too timid to suggest that he might not come back alive.

Right, a contemporary Mongolian woman with her hair styled for a festival. Below, veiled women on horseback.

Above, Mongolian women in the funeral procession of the Il-Khan Ghazan. Below, dancing women in fourteenth-century Samarkand, then the capital of Tamerlane's empire. Near right, a woman in her garden, as depicted in an Afghan miniature. Far right, a lady of rank at the court of Kublai Khan.

khan's policy to staff the bureaus of his government with foreigners—a sore point with the Chinese—Marco was offered a position as tax commissioner, with orders to travel through the empire, observe its workings, and report to the khan personally.

On his official trips through China, Marco noted the occupations of the inhabitants, the prices of goods, Chinese engineering projects, and local customs that struck him as bizarre, such as tattooing. At a seaport he observed that Chinese sailors tested the strength of the wind before embarking by sending a man up in a kite. He noted with revulsion that in Tibet the bodies of the dead were kept at home by their families until astrologers decreed the time was right for burial. For three years Marco served as governor of Hangchow, a commercial city on the Yangtze River. Traders in Hangchow conducted business in ten-story buildings, and Marco found that even the courtesans of the city were wealthy.

As a favorite of the khan, Marco frequently attended the festivals hosted by Kublai thirteen times a year. At the ceremonial banquets, the khan appeared in a costume of solid gold and the courtiers dressed in matching silk clothing provided by their host. The company was entertained by acrobats, magicians, and a trained tiger that loped through the throng to the khan's feet, where it loyally groveled. Every sum-

Above, Ulug-Beg (1394–1449), the ruler of Turkestan, administering justice. Ulug-Beg, whose Moslem name was Mehmet Turgay, was a grandson of Tamerlane. He ascended the throne of Turkestan in 1447—only to be killed two years later by his own son, who succeeded him.

Ulug-Beg was a cultured leader and a great lover of the arts; under his leadership Samarkand once again flourished as a center of learning. Left, a mosque built by Ulug-Beg in the center of the city. In addition to being a historian, theologian, and poet, Ulug-Beg was also a mathematician and astronomer; he ordered the construction of an observatory near Samarkand in the 1420s.

mer the khan indulged his passion for hunting. Setting out from Peking, he made his way to his favorite animal preserve with a portable palace of bamboo and an entourage of twenty thousand.

After seventeen years of service, Marco left China with his father and uncle on a voyage to Persia. During the trip, Kublai Khan died, and the Polos thought it best to proceed home to Italy in spite of a promise to return to China. In Italy, Marco wrote his travel account, *Description of the World,* which revealed the secrets of Asia—coal, asbestos, fantastic animals, and, most astounding of all, paper money—for the first time to an amazed Europe.

The magnificent empire described by Marco Polo began its decline in 1294 with the death of Kublai Khan, the last khan to preside over a unified Mongol Empire. Kublai's policy of staffing his government with foreigners and his favoritism toward wealthy traders and landowners had alienated the oppressed peasants, who rallied to native leaders advocating revolt against the barbarian ruling class. A series of uprisings led to the downfall of Kublai Khan's dynasty in China and the final expulsion of the Mongols in 1368.

As the Mongols were being driven from China, the western khanates, centered in Russia and Persia, entered a period of upheaval. After the death of Hulagu in 1265, Hulagu's son Abaka was forced into a series of civil wars with the Golden Horde and the khanate of Jagatai. Abaka's armies in Syria suffered a disastrous defeat at the hands of the Mamelukes in 1281. Later, after Abaka died of drunkenness, his son presided over a corrupt regime that exploited the Persian populace and oppressed the Moslems. The situation

Fighting continued between the inhabitants of the remnants of Tamerlane's empire and the Ottoman Turks in the sixteenth century. Below, a Turkish miniature depicting the siege of a fort by the Ottomans during the reign of the sultan Murad III (1546–1595).

was reversed in 1295, when Ghazan was elected khan in Persia. He embraced Islam, reformed the money system, and brought land into cultivation that had lain fallow since the ravages of Genghis Khan's war against Khwarizm. With Ghazan's early death in 1304 at the age of thirty-three, the western khanate again fell into chaos. Mongol nobles and tax takers pillaged the land, and the last descendant of Genghis Khan to hold the throne was poisoned.

In Russia the Golden Horde grew wealthy from trade with Egypt, Greece, and Genoa. Egyptian architects erected mosques and palaces in the Crimea, and the rich mosaics and frescoes that adorned the capital of Sarai have led modern Soviet archaeologists to dub the city the "Pompeii on the Volga." The Horde was temporarily weakened at the end of the thirteenth century by unsuccessful campaigns in Hungary and Poland and by internal warfare. The Russian princes became restive—twice the grand prince of Moscow inflicted defeats on the Mongols—but their lands were ravaged once again in 1382 in a campaign that matched Batu's in its savagery and thoroughness. At length the Russians were rescued, owing to, at least in part, a conqueror who had arisen in Samarkand to grasp the scepter of Genghis Khan.

The new conqueror was Tamerlane, who rallied the Turkish and Mongol remnants of the empire in Samarkand around 1370. His armies marched as far as the Black Sea, invaded India, and smashed the power of the Golden Horde, allowing the Russian princes, particularly the grand princes of Moscow, to throw off the Mongol yoke. Tamerlane had already defeated armies of the Ottoman Turks in Asia Minor and was laying plans for the conquest of China when he died in 1405, at the age of seventy. Tamerlane's successors lacked his ability, and the empire that had been won so quickly just as quickly disintegrated. In its wake the Ottoman Turks resumed their expansion and eventually wrested Egypt from the Mamelukes, taking Cairo in 1517. At about the same time, the

The last Timurid (descended from Tamerlane) rulers in Transoxiana and Iran were Husayn Baikara (1469–1506) and Badiaz Zaman (1506–1507), his son. Above, father and son making peace with each other after the son's attempt to rebel. The last survivors of the Mongol Empire lived in India under the Mogul dynasty. The Mongol book may be considered closed with the conquest of Bukhara in 1507 by the Uzbek ruler Shaybani. Right, a captured Mongol fighter.

Safawid dynasty established an independent state in Persia.

After the collapse of the Mongol Empire, the descendants of Genghis Khan's hordes in the Mongolian homeland returned to their internecine wars and occasional forays into China. For several hundred years the Chinese were able to play one tribe off against another to keep the Mongols from banding together. The eastern expansion of Russia placed the Mongols in the middle of the border struggles between Russia and China. Mongolia was governed by the Chinese until 1911, when the Mongols ousted their ancient enemies and proclaimed a free state—which lasted only eight years before the Chinese once again occupied the steppe. For the next three years, Mongolia was a battleground for the White and Red armies engaged in the Russian civil war. In 1924, Communist elements in Mongolia—perhaps with substantial Soviet assistance—set up the Mongolian People's Republic, which is closely allied today with the Soviet Union. The Soviets still regard the "Tatars" nervously and have discouraged what they call the "personality cult" of the "reactionary" Genghis Khan among modern Mongols. They have gone so far as to pressure the Mongolian government into withdrawing a stamp commemorating the eight-hundredth anniversary of the conqueror's birth.

The Russians have reason to remember with bitterness the centuries of Mongol tyranny; under the Mongols, the independence of the aristocrats, the towns, the Orthodox Church, and the peasants was inexorably eroded. In return for all they had extracted from Russia, the Mongols gave little if anything in return. As the nineteenth-century Russian poet Pushkin wrote: "The Tatars had nothing in common with the Moors. If they conquered Russia, they gave us neither algebra nor Aristotle!"

One unforeseen benefit of the Mongol rule in Asia was the opening of that continent to European missionaries and travelers. The visits of the Polos and innumerable other European traders during the reign of Kublai Khan aroused Europe's interest in the East, providing the stimulus for the great age of exploration that sought a water route to China and inadvertently found the New World.

The cultural and scientific legacy of the Mongols, however, was meager. In the arts the Mongols were, at best, more patrons than practitioners: They hired or dragooned foreign craftsmen for building projects since they themselves were amateurs at architecture, sculpture, and painting. Although Mongol funds built a university and an observatory, their achievements in scholarship and pure science were far less impressive than those of the Chinese or the Arabs.

The Mongols realized the value of commerce and abandoned their policy of exterminating "useless" farmers and townspeople only after the desperate intervention of Chinese and Persian advisers. The enlightened policies of Kublai Khan came late in the short history of the empire, and even his much-praised reign brought little prosperity to the peasant. The Mongols rebuilt many of the towns razed by war and revived some ravaged farming regions, but an equal number of towns and regions simply disappeared from the map after the destructive passage of a horde. It was impossible to rebuild a city after the population had been wiped out; as one chronicler wrote of a devastated Russian city: "No eye remained open to weep for the dead." In Iraq the Mongols destroyed an irrigation system that had taken centuries to build and returned much of the country to useless desert. The Mongols did much the same in Persia by altering the course of the Amu Darya to drown the survivors of a siege. Geographers believe that a branch of the river once emptied into the Caspian and watered a region that even today cannot be cultivated.

Military science was the one area in which the Mongols excelled. They were quick to master and improve Persian and Chinese siege equipment: catapults that could propel a twenty-five-pound object over one hundred and fifty yards, artillery that fired containers of burning tar, and bamboo rockets that were used to instill fear in the enemy. The Mongols, oddly enough, did not seem to grasp the destructive possibilities of gunpowder, which was in use in China as early as the ninth century. Though some writers have stated that the Mongols used gunpowder against the Poles and Hungarians, there is no evidence for this in the chronicles of these countries, which are full of detail about other Mongol military techniques. The Mongol generals, notably Subotai, mapped brilliant strategies that were studied by Napoleon and by English and German strategists before World War Two for their amazingly modern use of highly mobile units to surprise and outflank hostile formations. They were also pioneers in subduing civilian populations by terror and outright genocide: There were reports of 4,800,000 persons killed in the takeover of just four Middle Eastern cities. With some justice the Mongols will be remembered not for their astonishing empire but for their depredations, which the historian Edward Gibbon has referred to as events of "uncommon magnitude . . . in the history of blood."

The Mogul Expansion

When Zahir ud-Din Mohammed Baber, a descendant of the great conquerors Genghis Khan and Tamerlane, led his army from the plains of Transoxiana through the Hindu Kush into India in 1526, the Moguls were little more than a loosely knit group of adventurous warriors, living from battle to battle, uncertain of their future. Yet within the next seventy years, the dynasty founded by Baber would gain control of most of northern and western India and much of the central and eastern regions of the Indian subcontinent. Through resourceful military campaigns and progressive administrative reforms, the Moguls were able to transform themselves from one among many Moslem and Hindu aspirants, vying for control

of India, into an enduring political force that represented the diverse political and religious elements in their vast territories.

As the Moguls settled into the rich life of the north Indian plains, they refined the local culture according to their own tastes and traditions. By the early seventeenth century, reports of their military and artistic accomplishments had reached Europe by way of returning ambassadors and adventurers, merchants and missionaries. Poets, dancers, musicians, and artists from all over India, and Iran to the west, gravitated to the Mogul cities of Delhi, Fatehpur Sikri, Lahore, and Agra seeking imperial favor. In this way, a tribe of skilled warriors were destined to be remembered for their tolerance as patrons as well as their effectiveness as overlords of much of India.

The Moguls came from Transoxiana, an area of dry plains that sweep eastward from the Caspian and Aral seas, north of the towering mountains—the Pamirs, the Hindu Kush, the Karakoram—where Afghanistan, Pakistan, India, China, and the Soviet Union all meet. By the fifteenth century, many nomadic tribes lived on this semiarid plain, as did the inhabitants of various small states who were settled on scattered patches of watered land. These people were a mixture of Turkic and Mongol stock ("Mogul" is derived from the Persian word for Mon-

Preceding page, the Taj Mahal, the supreme symbol of Mogul India.

Kashmir was among the most coveted territories on the Indian subcontinent. Its gentle valleys (above) and its mild climate subjected it to incessant invasions from the fourteenth century on. Serving as the Moguls' favorite retreat, Kashmir harbored many warriors, including Baber, the dynasty's founder.

The villages of Kashmir (left) form a small part of the country's eighty-six thousand square miles. The rest is made up of mountains, narrow strips of fertile land, and lakes (below left) such as Lake Wular (above), the largest freshwater lake on the subcontinent. Along the lakes of Kashmir, at towns such as Srinagar, the Moguls built elaborate gardens with idyllic pools and marble pavilions.

gol) that had moved westward out of central Asia several centuries earlier. Moslem in religion and culture, and linked to the outside world by extensive trade routes crisscrossing their territory, they were receptive to influences from the more developed Moslem societies of Iran and Turkey and the neighboring Arab world.

One of the most fundamental of these inherited traditions was the Turkic spirit of conquest, exemplified by the grandiloquent words of the eleventh-century writer Mahmud Kashgari:

God has chosen the Turks as his own army, and settled them in the highest parts of the earth with the best air, that he may send them at his chosen time against any nation in the world.

To view the entire world as a potential conquest was an idea to which generations of the Moguls' ancestors had been exposed and by which future generations would uncompromisingly abide.

Life for these tribesmen was rigorous. Predominantly migratory, they lived armed, in the saddle, and close to nature. They constantly sought out water and grazing lands for the herds of sheep, camels, and horses on whose survival that of the tribes depended. Predatory animals, human enemies, and the danger

91

Immediately below, a stretch of the Ganges. Over fifteen hundred miles long, the river originates in the Himalayas near the eastern borders of Kashmir and flows eastward toward the Bay of Bengal, winding its way across India. Hindus believe that the Ganges is the holiest of all rivers and possesses extraordinary powers of purification. There are numerous holy bathing sites along its shores; the most famous are at Allahabad and Varanasi (Benares). Bottom, the dense vegetation of the eastern Himalayas, whose valleys resemble tropical rain forests. In contrast, the western Himalayas have dry, rock-walled valleys that are uninhabitable. Right, the terraced fields of Kashmir where rice, barley, wheat, and sugar cane are grown.

of drought were ever present. It was a demanding and ruthless life in which military virtues were cultivated: Discipline and cohesiveness, courage and energy were requisites for survival; leadership was based as much on ability as on family connections; skill in diplomacy and stratagem was highly prized.

For all its militarism, tribal society was not exclusively masculine. Women played a significant role, for the elaborate rituals guarding the seclusion of women in the more conservative and sedentary Moslem societies had little place in this nomadic world. Sharing rather than private ownership was the norm, and both men and women participated in informal discussions of issues affecting the welfare of the tribe.

As the nomads migrated from summer pastures in the hills and lower mountain slopes to winter grazing on the plains, they encountered the small agricultural

states of the fertile lowlands. These states had sprung up at oases or along the waterways that expanded each year as the spring thaws drained the snowy mountain slopes. Irrigation systems carried these waters into small garden plots around the towns, where fruits and vegetables grew in abundance. The people of these settlements were prosperous and civilized compared to the nomads; their cultural activities flourished at the various minor courts, which patronized poets, painters, and storytellers.

The most famous of these cities were Samarkand, Bukhara, Herāt, and Fergana—places the nomads associated with ease and luxury, the delights of abundant water and verdant gardens. The frequent wars between these states and the nomads, therefore, had the special viciousness of rivalry between haves and have-nots. Here, the nomadic horsemen sacked with particular zest when the opportunity arose.

The political equilibrium of these oasis states was unstable. Dominance depended upon possession of arable land—which was in limited supply. A drought, the incursion of a new tribe, or an alliance by marriage could upset the balance, provoking violent struggles for supremacy. Furthermore, under Islamic doctrine, no leader could appoint his successor, nor was the law of primogeniture (by which the eldest son automatically inherited all of his father's land) strictly followed. Rather, each son had absolute equality of rights. Though one son might have an obvious edge over his siblings in terms of age, ability, or reputation, enabling him to seize power upon his father's demise, as a rule the death of a king brought on plotting and maneuvering until one new leader could emerge victorious.

This typically Turkic attitude toward succession was yet another dimension of the Moguls' cultural heritage, a heritage that was to play a tremendous role in the conquest and governing of India. The ancestors of the Moguls were few in number, but disciplined in war, cohesive in organization, aggressive in temperament, ruthless in battle, and flexible in policy. The Moguls were to need all these attributes as they prepared to descend into India.

The first to lead his followers southward was the notoriously fierce warrior Tamerlane (Timur the Lame). With only a small force, he swept over the mountains of the Hindu Kush in 1398; yet he overcame all before him, winning many battles, sacking town after town, and capturing the leading city in India—Delhi. The rewards—and the slaughter—were immense. But for Tamerlane this was merely an expedition, not a campaign of conquest. He retired to Samarkand in 1399, taking with him masses of slaves, especially skilled craftsmen whom he put to work beautifying his capital and enhancing its prestige.

Tamerlane's raid had both immediate and far-reaching consequences. It provided his successors with a claim, albeit weak, to northern India. It demonstrated that Indian armies, despite their much-feared elephants, were too loosely organized and poorly trained to withstand the Mogul forces. And it spread word throughout Transoxiana and central Asia of India's wealth, of the rich future that other adventurers might expect from a successful campaign south of the mountains.

Tamerlane's descendant Zahir ud-Din Mohammed Baber was encouraged by the early expeditions of his predecessors into India. In 1494, at the age of eleven, Baber had come into the leadership of the area around Fergana in Transoxiana; a few years later, he conquered, then lost, the city of Samarkand. The early years of his life were dominated by such short-lived military engagements. His defeats were the defeats of one small band of men by another; losses were rarely large and never devastating.

Moving south, he crossed the Hindu Kush and conquered Kabul in eastern Afghanistan in 1504. His resources were pitiful, as he admitted in his memoirs:

> The followers who still adhered to my fortunes, great and small, exceeded 200 and fell short of 300. The greater part of them were on foot with sandals on their feet, clubs in their hands, and long frocks over their shoulders. Such was their distress that amongst us all we had only two tents.

Undaunted, Baber led his first raid into India in 1505, along the banks of the Indus River. Two years

Left, the Gaurav Stambha, or pillar of fame, at Chitor, whose richly carved walls depict various Hindu gods. Built between 1440 and 1448 by Raja Kumbha, the tower rises to a height of 120 feet. Although it is unknown why this tower was constructed—some scholars believe it served to commemorate a victory and others argue that its function was strictly religious—the Hindu custom of building columns or towers in India dates back to at least the third century B.C. The Moslems also had a tradition of building towers or minarets, usually to mark military victories.

Above, a fortified Bahmani palace. The large, roughly hewn stones of its walls are typical of such fortifications. The Bahmanids (1347–1527), whose capital was at Gulbarga in the southern Deccan, were one of the last Moslem sultanates to resist the Moguls. Right, the tomb of Isa Khan, one of Afghan king Sher Shah's generals. This tomb (ca. 1545–1547), like all Sur dynasty tombs, is an octagonal structure built of carefully shaped stone. The chatris, or pavilions, along the tomb's upper walls later became common architectural features of Mogul tombs.

Each of the deities in the Hindu pantheon has several distinctive characteristics. Shiva (left) is seen here in his four-headed, ten-armed incarnation. He wears a necklace of skulls and is armed with a sword, bowl, conch shell, shield, trident, snake, and mace (spiked club), symbols of his destructive powers. He also holds a lotus blossom and a ring. Right, Brahma riding on his goose Hamsa. He usually is represented with four heads, though here he is seen with only three.

Immediately below, Krishna, the eighth incarnation of Vishnu, renowned for his strength, shrewdness, and love affairs (he supposedly had some 16,000 wives who bore him a total of 180,000 sons). He is frequently shown dancing with the gopis, or cowgirls, with whom he cavorted as a youth. Bottom, Ganesa, the elephant-headed god, attended by maidservants who offer him his favorite fruits. Right, Vishnu and his consort Lakshmi, goddess of Fortune and Prosperity, riding on Vishnu's charger Garuda.

Hinduism

Hinduism, the religion of the majority of the Moguls' subjects, is based on the idea that time is a never-ending cycle of creation and destruction. Hindus believe in many gods, the most important of which are Brahma (the creator), Vishnu (the preserver), and Shiva (the destroyer).

Hindu society is divided into four major castes, believed to have come into being when the lord Purusha was sacrificed and a different caste sprang from each part of his body. They consist of the Brahmins, or priests; the Kshatriyas, or warriors; the Vaisyas, or farmers and merchants; and the Sudras, or serfs and laborers.

During the first Moslem invasions of India in the twelfth and thirteenth centuries, Hindu temples were destroyed and the people were forced to pay a head tax. The Moguls, however, under Emperor Akbar (reigned 1556–1605), recognized the contributions of the Hindu population and exempted Hindus from such discriminatory decrees.

later he struck again, then reversed direction, joining with the Iranians in winning some victories in western Afghanistan. In the face of eventual defeat, however, Baber withdrew to Kabul in 1514 to consolidate his forces. Then he turned again to north India, where the prospects were tempting. That area, ruled as the sultanate of Delhi since the fourteenth century, was a long, narrow corridor of land extending along the Ganges and Jama valleys from the far northwest frontier to the borders of Bengal in the east. The sultans were Moslems of Afghan origin, and their control depended on their skill in cajoling and manipulating an indigenous group of quasi-independent governors and other powerful Hindu nobles. In 1517 a new sultan, Ibrahim, came to power. His tyrannical rule provoked his nobles to rise in rebellion. The subsequent confusion was viewed with satisfaction by the leaders of the neighboring states, especially those of Rajasthan, to the west of Delhi. Ruled by the Rajputs—Hindu warriors renowned for their fierce fighting abilities—Rajasthan had in the past successfully resisted incursions from the Delhi sultans.

Baber, raiding into this already volatile situation in 1519 and 1520, accepted an alliance by the rebels opposing Ibrahim. Several minor victories then set the stage for the climactic battle of Panipat, near Delhi, on April 20, 1526.

Accounts of the numbers involved at Panipat vary considerably. It is clear, though, that Baber's forces were vastly outnumbered by those of Ibrahim. Ibrahim commanded as many as a thousand elephants, which carried on their backs *howdahs,* or armored gondolas, for archers and other soldiers. These lumbering beasts ordinarily were used to break the enemy line, but the noise and fury of battle sometimes made them uncontrollable, as dangerous to their masters as to the enemy.

Though Baber possessed primitive firearms—the first to be introduced into India, probably imported from Turkey—it is doubtful that artillery played a decisive role in the battle. Baber's principal advantage was based on his strongly fortified position as well as his disciplined and tightly organized troops, which had a decisive edge over the loosely massed forces of Sultan Ibrahim. Mogul fire brought the charging cavalry and elephants to a standstill, and as the Moguls skillfully maneuvered their reserves, their cavalry surged forward, forcing Ibrahim's men into a tightening circle. Casualties mounted. Ibrahim himself was killed, and his army broke and fled, suffering heavily as the Mogul cavalry pursued. Baber soon secured the cities of Delhi and Agra (about one hundred miles southeast of Delhi) and was proclaimed emperor of his new lands. The sultanate of Delhi had

Baber, the founder of the Mogul dynasty, was a great statesman and poet. His memoir, the Baber Nama, *provides a detailed account of life in India during the early sixteenth century. Attending the durbar (above), or formal audience, was one of his many daily obligations. Below, a battle scene depicting Baber's ancestors, from a sixteenth-century Persian manuscript.*

Baber (right) was not only a gifted statesman and poet but a fearsome warrior as well. His ancestors included Genghis Khan and Tamerlane (Timur the Lame), two of central Asia's greatest warriors. In 1494, at the age of eleven, Baber inherited the region of Fergana, to the east of Samarkand. By 1525 he had already made five expeditions into India through the Hindu Kush. In posthumous portraits, the emperor is always depicted as a trim, lightly bearded man with a mustache. The gentle features of his face suggest the more literary aspects of his character.

fallen, and the princes of north India suddenly were confronted with a formidable new leader.

Although Baber had won this battle, the future was still far from certain. Sultan Ibrahim had many rivals whom Baber inherited along with the sultan's land. These opponents included much of the local nobility and, most important, the powerful Rajput states of Rajasthan. Baber sent his eldest son, Humayun, to crush the nobles while he himself took on the Rajputs in a short campaign that culminated in the battle of Khanua, near Agra, on March 16, 1527. Again, though vastly outnumbered, the Mogul forces emerged victorious, having driven the Rajputs from the field of battle.

The victory at Panipat had toppled a dynasty; that at Khanua achieved far more. The legend of Rajput invincibility was destroyed and the Mogul presence on Indian soil confirmed. Yet a major problem remained: the inability of the Moguls to consolidate politically what they had won in battle. Baber did not live long enough to entrench himself firmly in India. His successes were military rather than political. By winning one last campaign against a large Bengali force at Gogra, near Patna, on May 6, 1529, he extended Mogul control far to the east, through the region of Bihar to the very borders of Bengal.

Ironically, he viewed the country he had conquered as a poor prize. Baber—and for that matter his successors—never lost his ties to his distant homeland of Transoxiana. The lure of Samarkand persisted, and Baber sent Humayun on a final, unsuccessful military expedition to take the city. Samarkand was, after all, Tamerlane's capital, the chief city of Transoxiana, the seat of culture and government, and a prize that had eluded Baber. By contrast the dusty towns of northern India (Hindustan) over which he now ruled

Battles in India during the sixteenth century were hard fought. Fortresses of heavy sandstone blocks were almost impregnable, and intense, often prolonged, attacks (above left) were necessary to gain entrance. When repeated assaults proved unsuccessful, the attackers often resorted to deceitful tactics to dupe the enemy into opening the gates. Left, skilled archers, from a fifteenth-century Persian manuscript. Mogul archers led the troops and often decided the outcome of crucial battles. By the 1520s the Moguls had introduced firearms and cannons to India, vastly altering the nature of warfare (right).

held little attraction for him. Baber wrote of the place with some bitterness:

> Hindustan is a country of few charms. Its people have no good looks; of social intercourse, paying and receiving visits there is none; of genius and capacity none; of manners none; in handicraft and work there is no form of symmetry, method or quality; there are no good horses, no good dogs; no grapes, muskmelons or first rate fruits, no ice or cold water, no good bread or cooked food in the bazaar, no hot baths, no colleges, no candles, torches, or candlesticks.

When he died on December 26, 1530, Baber turned his back on India as he had not been able to do in his life. He requested that he be buried in Kabul, in Afghanistan, and his wish was carried out.

Humayun, now twenty-three, became *padshah*, or emperor, succeeding his father. Though the Indian nobility had grudgingly accepted the great—and dangerous—Baber, they were prepared to assert themselves against his heir. Humayun was amiable but irresolute, possessing a disposition to which both opium and alcohol appear to have contributed. Soon after he came to power, the various courts of northern India began to seethe with conspiracies, schemes, and rebellion. Yet the Mogul military system functioned as effectively for Humayun as it had for his father. A rebellion instigated by his principal rival, the sultan of Gujarat, on the west coast of India, was quelled temporarily in 1535. Gujarat, however, remained a major source of opposition, in part because Humayun's lethargy kept him from capitalizing politically on his military victories. Moreover, the population of Gujarat was firmly united against the Moguls (who were evicted in 1536).

Bihar, in northeast India, presented a comparable problem to the Moguls. Its leader, Sher Khan (known

The Rajput chieftains, who controlled most of northwestern India, were archetypical warriors whose lives were consumed with ruling, hunting, and loving. Violent differences of opinion were frequent, and the various clans, such as the Sesodias and Haras, were almost constantly at war. Most of the year the Rajput chieftains lived in massive citadels, one of the most impressive being the Man Mandir (above right) at Gwalior. Built by Raja Man Singh ca. 1510, its sandstone walls are nearly one hundred feet high and were once richly inlaid with colored tiles. Although the citadel is now abandoned, its massive walls and turrets give it a sense of permanence. Right, a relief depicting battle and hunting scenes at Vijayanagar, the capital of the Deccan. These lively figures commemorate Krishna Raya's victory over the region of Orissa in 1513.

after 1540 as Sher Shah), came from a background closely resembling that of the Mogul leaders: He too was a foreigner, his grandfather having left Afghanistan for India to make his fortune under the sultanate of Delhi. A political opportunist, he at first joined forces with the Moguls as their fortunes rose. It was obvious to his new allies, though, that his sole concern was his own future. While the fighting in Gujarat was distracting the Moguls, Sher Khan set about increasing his own power at the expense of Bengal (which he eventually conquered in early 1539). In 1537, Humayun attacked the upstart Sher Khan on his home territory. The campaign was a disaster for the Moguls. Abandoned by his allies—including his own half brothers—his lines of communication to Delhi and Agra cut by Sher Khan, Humayun was isolated militarily and diplomatically. The morale of his

Baber's memoir records an almost endless litany of battles, many of which were depicted in the Baber Nama. *The defenders are invariably shown at the moment the enemy has been put to flight, and meticulous care has been taken with detail. In the painting above, for instance, each soldier's garments are distinct; faces, while generalized, are animated, giving the picture a sense of urgency; and individual gestures are precisely rendered. This attention to detail even extends to the fortress in the background, in which each stone is clearly visible.*

troops was falling rapidly. At last Humayun attempted to negotiate for peace with his enemy. In response Sher Khan caught the Mogul army off guard with a surprise attack at daybreak. The army was totally annihilated, and Humayun himself barely escaped. Though he eventually formed a new army, he was defeated yet again by Sher Khan in the Ganges valley in May of 1540.

Facing capture or assassination, and with his followers deserting en masse, Humayun fled once again. He trekked north to Lahore, drawn back to Afghanistan and the plains beyond. Humayun tried desperately to unite his half brothers and other local leaders against Sher Shah, who had proclaimed himself king.

But he was again unsuccessful, for all potential allies were now making their peace with the new emperor. With only a handful of followers, the deposed ruler pushed south to the bleak desert of Sind in western India. It was there, in October of 1542, that his empress gave birth to a son, Akbar.

Although his empire had virtually been destroyed, there was still sufficient hope for recovery. In January 1544, Humayun, his family, and his small entourage reached Iran. There they were warmly welcomed by Shah Tahmasp, who gave the fugitives a home and eventually provided Humayun with an army. Backed by his new-found allies, the emperor began to show unprecedented energy and skill. That same year he led his army back into Afghanistan, where he defeated his half brothers in battle. From this base of operations he now contemplated the reconquest of northern India. This time his prospects seemed promising. Though Sher Shah had been a relatively just ruler, his death in 1545 triggered several debilitating wars of succession from which no new leader had emerged.

Seizing this opportunity to attack, Humayun entered Delhi in 1555 after a long series of military victories and secured the city. He died suddenly only months later, but the momentum of his return was sustained after his death. With the help of a loyal corps of commanders and advisers, his young son, Akbar, came to power.

Akbar, unlike his father and grandfather, had been born in India. He was thus the first of the Mogul emperors to view India not as a potential conquest but as his home. Virtually a child when he came to the throne in early 1556, Akbar ruled the region around Delhi under the governorship of Bairam Khan, who had been one of Humayun's most trusted advisers. As usual there were rivals for the throne, the two most troublesome of whom were the Moslem leaders Sikandar Shah of the Punjab (a neighboring region northwest of Delhi) and Adil Shah, an Afghani claimant.

Bairam Khan and Akbar decided to march first against Sikandar Shah. During their absence from

Delhi, a Hindu named Hemu who had served under Adil Shah seized the capital, Delhi. When this news reached Akbar, he promptly returned and on November 5, 1556, led the Mogul army to meet Hemu and his troops at Panipat, the site of Baber's great victory. During the fighting Hemu was killed and his army scattered. The young emperor regained his throne. Not satisfied with one victory, Akbar returned to the Punjab in pursuit of Sikandar Shah, defeating him as well in 1557. Akbar's good fortune persisted when, that same year, his other rival, Adil Shah, was killed by Bengali troops in a battle. Within a year and a half of assuming the throne, Akbar found himself securely entrenched at Delhi.

It would be a mistake to assume that these early successes were due solely to a fortuitous combination of luck and good advice. Akbar was a man of ex-

Below, the emperor Baber dictating his memoir, from an early seventeenth-century painting. He is attended by two servants and a scribe, whose writing implements would have included an assortment of reed pens and specially prepared inks. Right, Baber crossing a river from a late seventeenth-century copy of the Baber Nama. *The emperor's raft, supported by large pontoons, is guided by a team of expert swimmers.*

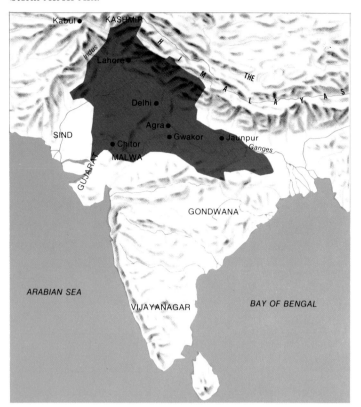

The sultanate of Delhi in 1398

From the early thirteenth century, when the sultanate of Delhi was created, until the fifteenth century, the sultanate had been the center of Moslem rule in northern India. During the late thirteenth and fourteenth centuries, under the rule of the Khiljis (1290–1320) and the Tughlaks (1321–1414), the kingdom had been expanded southward toward Vijayanagar. By the end of the fourteenth century, however, these vast holdings proved too much for the sultanate, and a number of independent kingdoms were established. Tamerlane's sack of Delhi in 1398 and concurrent political unrest further reduced the sultanate's lands. In 1500 the sultanate stretched only from Lahore in the north to Chitor in the southwest and Bihar in the east. Ruled by the weak Lodi dynasty (Moslems of Afghan descent), the politically crippled sultanate was unable to exert much power beyond the Delhi area.

The Mogul Empire in 1775

Throughout the late seventeenth and eighteenth centuries the Mogul Empire witnessed a number of momentous changes, the most significant being Aurangzeb's departure from the liberal social and religious tolerance that had been crucial to the formation of the empire. The aftermath of Aurangzeb's futile campaign in the Deccan further weakened the Moguls' dominion. By 1775 the entire Deccan had been lost to the Marathas and Bengal, and parts of the east and west coasts to the British. As a result, the Moguls were left with little more than a small area around Delhi.

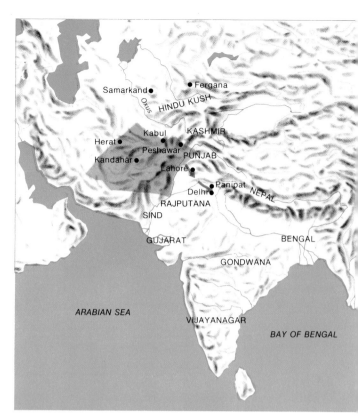

The conquests of Baber

Forced in 1504 to flee the fertile plains of his native Fergana, Baber settled in Kabul. After several unsuccessful attempts to regain his kingdom, he focused his attention on Delhi. From 1519 until 1524 he embarked on four raids across the Hindu Kush into India. During the same period, he extended his lands to the west, capturing Kandahār in 1522. Then in 1525 he made his final descent into India, where he seized Delhi from the Lodis, and thus secured a permanent foothold in India.

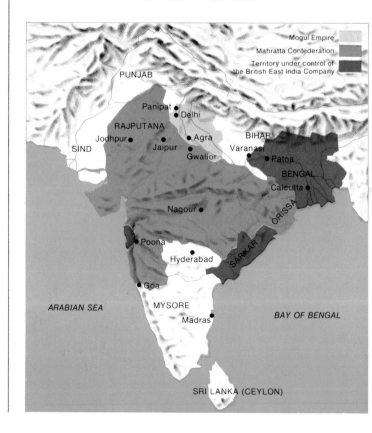

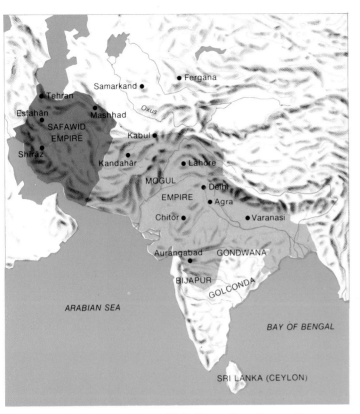

The Empire at Akbar's death

When Akbar ascended the throne in 1556, the Mogul Empire encompassed little more than the area surrounding the city of Delhi. By 1570, however, Rajasthan was under Mogul control; Bengal met the same fate by 1580. During the late 1580s and 90s Akbar pushed northward into Kashmir, westward into Sind, and southward into the Deccan. At the emperor's death in 1605 the Mogul Empire comprised almost all the lands from the Hindu Kush to Bengal and from Kabul to Bijapur.

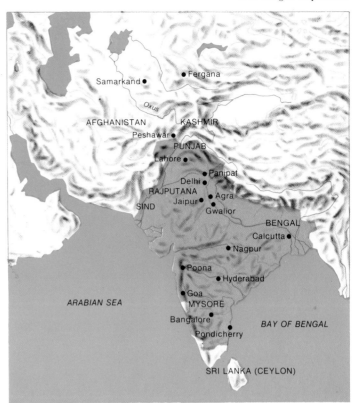

The Empire at Aurangzeb's death

The empire Aurangzeb claimed for himself in 1658 had not changed significantly since the death of his great-grandfather Akbar. Both Aurangzeb's father and grandfather had attempted to extend the empire to include all of the Deccan but neither was successful. In 1680, Aurangzeb undertook a massive campaign to accomplish this task. By 1689 the rebellious kingdoms of Bijapur and Golconda had fallen to the Moguls. Aurangzeb's efforts, however, were met by the fierce resistance of the Maratha tribesmen. Fighting on native territory, they forced Aurangzeb into a lengthy and costly war that lasted until his death in 1707.

Although Aurangzeb had greatly enlarged his kingdom in the Deccan, the victory was hollow—the crusade brought the empire to the brink of bankruptcy.

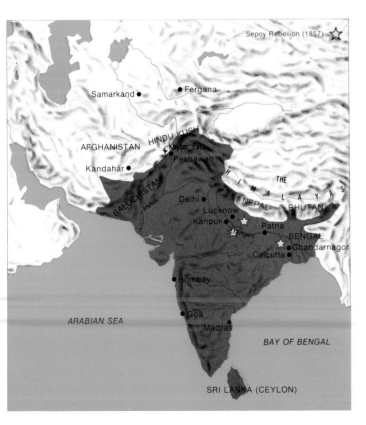

The British Empire in India

In 1857 the native troops of the East India Company's army revolted in Bengal. Prompted by a rumor that the East India Company had issued cartridges coated with animal fat, the mutiny rapidly spread throughout much of northern India. The underlying cause of the insurrection, however, lay in Hindu and Moslem resentment of the company's annexation of their lands. Despite several initial losses, the British quelled the rebellion by March 1858. Reaction in England to the mutiny was so strong that it brought about an abrupt transfer of power and control of India from the East India Company to the crown. Until 1947, when India gained its independence, Britain's rule over India was supreme.

traordinary character. Whereas his father had been quiet, contemplative, almost scholarly in his interests, Akbar was a born leader.

It was Akbar who, more than any ruler, shaped the Mogul Empire. He formulated and developed almost all the major administrative and social policies that would be put into practice by his descendants. It was his political inspiration that gave the empire its stability and its modus operandi. As long as his successors adhered to his policies, the empire prospered.

Akbar was a man of tremendous vitality. As a child, he enjoyed all kinds of rigorous physical activity—riding wild camels, wrestling, hunting. He did not at first share his father's interest in literature and poetry but came to appreciate them in his later years. Although as a royal prince he was taught the basics of reading and writing, he never seems to have been able

Above left, Humayun, the son and successor of Baber, from a late sixteenth-century copy of the History of the Timurids (Tatikh-i Timuriya). *Upon acceding to his father's throne in 1530, Humayun was beset by countless rebellions. In 1544 he was forced to flee to Iran where he remained until 1554. Left, Humayun's tomb in Delhi, begun in 1560 by his widow Sahibah Begum and completed nine years later. This large red sandstone structure is mounted on a plinth, or platform, in the center of a large garden. Its octagonal shape, graceful lines, and paradisiacal setting anticipate the design and surroundings of the Taj Mahal. Above, the main gate to the Puranaquila, a citadel in Delhi, built ca. 1550. Its sandstone walls and inlaid marble decorations are almost identical to those of Humayun's tomb; triangles forming the Shield of Abraham are found on both structures.*

to use these skills, possibly because he suffered from dyslexia. Nevertheless, his mind was extremely sharp, always capable of grasping facts quickly. He was particularly adept at understanding the crux of any situation and acting decisively—two abilities his father had lacked. These qualities enabled him, in the span of twenty years, to create out of a military conquest a stable, efficiently administered empire. He was, according to his biographer, Abu-l Fazl, a ruler blessed with charisma, wisdom, strength, and an unerring faith in himself and his empire.

Having emerged victorious in facing his earliest rivals, the young Akbar dismissed one adviser and executed another, setting himself a grander goal: the subjugation of Rajasthan. Rajasthan had stood for centuries as the bitter opponent of virtually every aspirant to the control of India. The kingdom, made up of the formidable Rajput states, presented dangerous opposition to a relatively inexperienced emperor ruling in a time of political instability. But expansion into this territory was vital to Akbar's survival, for without securing its western flanks, the empire would always be vulnerable to attack from marauders.

Akbar also needed to keep his troops occupied, since he could not afford to risk the consequences of

Sher Shah was an Afghan who, in 1540, founded a short-lived dynasty in India when he forced Humayun to flee Delhi. His tomb (below) at Sasaram is a multilevel octagonal building situated in the middle of an artificial lake. Its dome is over 150 feet high.

an idle force: restlessness, disenchantment, even rebellion. He expressed his own thoughts on the subject bluntly: "A monarch should be ever intent on conquest, otherwise his neighbors will rise in arms against him. The army should be exercised in warfare lest from want of training they become self-indulgent."

The emperor's task of expanding into Rajput territory was made easier by the inability of the Rajputs to form a unified alliance. At length, Akbar emerged victorious from two sieges in the Rajput highlands. The first was the siege of Chitor (1567–1568), a barbaric onslaught that is remembered through history as a symbol of Mogul ruthlessness. Akbar's troops systematically undermined and bombarded the battlements of the city as a preamble to a final bloody assault on Chitor. Some thirty thousand of the helpless enemy were massacred. After the victory Akbar forbade any reconstruction. The devastated town was to remain in ruins for generations as a reminder of what would happen to those who dare to resist the advances of the Moguls.

The siege of Ranthambhor (1569) taught a different lesson: Akbar could display generosity and restraint, if it suited his needs. The Rajput commander of the town proved amenable, ready to consider Akbar's terms—and his bribes. So there was neither heavy fighting nor a massacre, neither vengeance nor glory, but an amicable settlement. Many of the Rajput princes were given lucrative positions in Akbar's administration, and many of their princesses were dispatched to his harem as wives. The Rajput nobility was admitted freely to the Mogul military organization, in which they rose according to their merits.

Akbar's alliance with the Rajputs was personal as well as political. In 1562 he married the daughter of the raja of Amber, one of the most powerful Rajput chiefs, and sealed an alliance that brought him the

Left, the siege of Chitor, from a late sixteenth-century manuscript. One of Akbar's most important military victories, this siege lasted from October 20, 1567, to February 23, 1568. Akbar was so enraged by the fierce resistance offered by the townspeople that he massacred over thirty thousand of the defenders. Above right, Akbar with musicians and courtiers. Although illiterate, Akbar took an avid interest in literature, philosophy, poetry, music, and dance, and summoned leading musicians, artists, and scholars to his court throughout his reign. Right, a detail of the siege at Ranthambhor (1569), from a late sixteenth-century copy of the Akbar Nama, *Akbar's memoir. Unlike Chitor, this was an easy victory for the Moguls.*

Preceding page, the Diwan-i-Khas, or private audience hall, at Fatehpur Sikri, a town begun by Akbar in 1571. When Akbar moved his court to Lahore in 1584, the building and the town were abandoned. Above, flowers in the Shalimar gardens at Lahore. This magnificent complex built by Shah Jahan (reigned 1627–1658) contains numerous white marble pavilions (right) and waterfalls and waterways (below right). Far right, a miniature depicting laborers at work on a pool similar to the ones at Lahore.

benefits of Rajput military skill, administrative abilities, and prestige.

His marriage to a Hindu princess also signaled his emerging policy of religious tolerance. Although Moslem, he granted concessions to the Hindus and offered royal patronage to Hindu artists, musicians, and civil servants. In 1563, he incurred the enmity of Orthodox Moslems at court by revoking the *jizya,* a tax paid by those outside of the Islamic faith. Akbar's gesture of tolerance toward the Hindus was motivated, at least in part, by political expediency: The Moguls ruled as a Moslem minority in the midst of a Hindu nation. Without the cooperation and support of the Hindus on all levels, the Moguls stood little chance of transforming themselves from a force of occupation into the rulers of a cohesive empire.

After subduing the Rajputs, Akbar turned his sights east, to Bihar and Bengal, which had broken away from Akbar's overlordship, setting a challenge too dangerous to be ignored. In March of 1575 a strong Mogul army went forth to conquer and punish

at the battle of Tukaroi; yet here the Moguls narrowly emerged victorious. As at Chitor, the Moguls reacted to near defeat by massacring their prisoners and displaying the severed heads on towers, in the style of their ancestor Tamerlane. While the Moguls had become refined and sophisticated in matters of art and religion, the barbarous spirit of their forebearers still survived in war.

To be fair, such savagery was rare. There was none, for example, in Akbar's remarkably swift conquest of Gujarat (1572–1573). With this victory he gained outlets on the Arabian Sea, facilitating the pilgrimage to Mecca of his Moslem subjects while opening his empire to sustained contact with Africa, the Arab world, and even Europe. Portuguese trading settlements—transmitting Western ideas and technology as well as goods—were established on India's west coast. And occasionally European merchants, adventurers, and especially Catholic missionaries were received at Akbar's court.

Through successful military campaigns in the

1580s and early 1590s, Akbar gained all the far western regions of India and much of Afghanistan, again without excessive bloodshed. The emperor subdued his rebellious half brother Hakim in Afghanistan during 1581, suppressed all opposition in Kashmir, north of Delhi, during 1585 to 1586, conquered Sind in 1591, pushed farther west into Baluchistan in 1595, and in the same year pressed deeper into Afghanistan by acquiring Kandahār.

During this period Akbar and his court were constantly on the move. By the end of the sixteenth century Akbar had swept up all the states of the broad zone that lay between Iran and Mogul India. To have advanced farther would have thrown him into serious conflict with Iran, itself a first-class military power, and would have dangerously overextended his territorial ambitions in the west of his empire. Searching for a new direction for his expansionist energies, Akbar looked to the south.

The Deccan, in south-central India, was a desolate area broken up by ranges of rocky hills and numerous

Above, an exterior view of a pavilion and an interior view of the Palace of Mirrors, both at the fort in Lahore. Built by Akbar at the end of the sixteenth century, the fort is constructed on the ruins of an earlier fortress. The main part of the fort consists of red sandstone; the towers and portals are decorated with mosaics and tiles. Contrasted with the extensively decorated interiors of many of the pavilions, the façades project a stark harshness. Left, a detail of one of the courtyards at the fort. Right, the marble-screened interior of one of the buildings at Lahore.

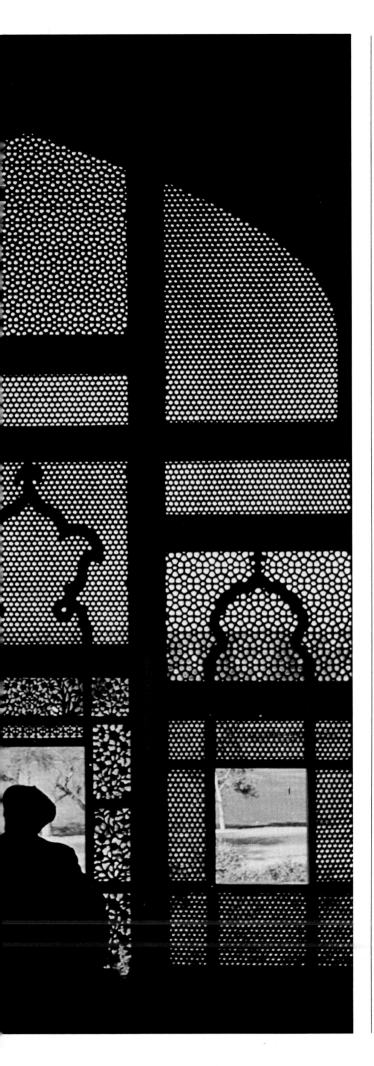

valleys. Communications were difficult, food and fodder limited. This was a terrain well suited to ambushes and skirmishes, a region where a large army was likely to find meager supplies—and meager success. It was hardly a favorable environment for the Mogul military, which relied on cavalry attacks over open ground and on ponderous siege artillery. Yet this was the area that Akbar invaded. To the frustration of the Mogul forces, the local princes responded to the incursion with hit-and-run tactics rather than the pitched battles at which the Moguls excelled. As a result the Moguls' forays into the Deccan proved, at best, indecisive.

Akbar personally conducted these military campaigns, for he rarely delegated to others the decision-making powers granted him by Mogul tradition. Hence the administrative hierarchy, lacking powers of its own, could not simply remain behind in Agra (which Akbar had established as capital in the early 1560s) conducting the daily business of collecting taxes and arbitrating judicial matters. Instead senior officials accompanied the emperor on his travels across the subcontinent. And because the Mogul elite took the pursuit of pleasure seriously, luxury was in as much demand on the march as in the capital. Accordingly, the military and administrative troops were joined by contingents of wives, children, servants, advisers, craftsmen, artists, musicians, and other entertainers.

To transport and feed this horde of camp followers, to rule the rest of India from isolated and hostile regions, and to control potential dissidents in distant reaches of the empire were tasks requiring almost superhuman ability. Remarkably Akbar managed it all.

By the last quarter of the sixteenth century, Akbar had gained dominance over much of the Indian subcontinent. But sheer military might was not enough to ensure political stability. Administrative reforms were needed to preserve order in the vast and growing empire. As the emperor's court increased in size, so did the needs for money to support the bureaucracy. Akbar therefore instituted a system under which the empire was divided into crown lands, quasi-military subdivisions called *jagirs,* for the purpose of collecting revenues. Each jagir was managed by a nobleman responsible for gathering the area's rent and who received a salary for his service. This need for revenue-producing land may account for, in part, Akbar's expansionist policies, under which he constantly attempted to subdue the Deccan, despite the hostility of the terrain and the excellent defenses of the local tribesmen.

Akbar was a social reformer as well as an innova-

tive administrator. In addition to extending religious tolerance to the Hindus, he attempted to ban child marriages and the infamous practice of *sati*, the immolation of Hindu wives on their husbands' funeral pyres. He also restricted prostitution to specific quarters of the towns, in effect establishing "red-light" districts, and he attempted to regulate gambling.

The emperor's legal reforms were extremely important, as they formed the statutory basis of the empire. However, they also created many of the tensions that led to the empire's eventual dissolution. Before Akbar's reign, the legal and religious authority of the empire had resided theoretically in the *ulema*, an Orthodox Moslem body. In 1579 Akbar formalized his independence from the ulema, issuing a decree of imperial infallibility called the *mahzar*. In effect this decree made Akbar the sole judge of legal and religious matters, limited the powers of the Orthodox Moslems, and enabled the emperor to take full control of his lands. It also served to further antagonize the Orthodox element at court, already alienated by Akbar's open policies toward the Hindus. Because of his unique position and his firm control over the military, Akbar was able to dominate this faction. Later rulers were not so fortunate.

Akbar's religious policies can best be seen in the context of his lifelong quest for religious understanding. From an early age Akbar was deeply interested in philosophical and theological matters. Abu-l Fazl even recorded occasions on which the emperor seemed to have lapsed into a spiritual trance. At his court at Fatehpur Sikri (established outside of Agra as the new capital in 1571 and abandoned for Lahore in 1584), the emperor gathered around him theologians of various faiths—Jesuits from Portuguese Goa, Zoroastrians from Iran, Jews, and Hindus—and he joined them in lively debate.

Akbar even formulated his own religion—the Din-i Ilahi, or Religion of God. As a faith, it was vague and

Left, one of the pavilions on each side of the entrance to the Lahore mosque of Wazir Khan (a governor of the city), begun in 1634. The walls of this building are covered with richly decorated enamel tiles. Center right and right, details of tile work in the Palace of Mirrors and in the Shish Mahal, both located in Lahore.

Top right, the marble courtyard and cenotaph (monument) atop Akbar's tomb at Sikandra. The first three stories of the tomb are made of red sandstone and form an imposing base for the delicately carved courtyard above.

The Safawids

The Safawid dynasty, founded in 1501 by Shah Ismail, ruled over most of Iran and Afghanistan until its fall in 1722. Friendly relations between the Safawids and the Moguls usually prevailed, as in the 1540s, when Shah Tahmasp, Shah Ismail's son and successor, allowed Mogul emperor Humayun to take refuge in Iran. While there, the exiled ruler hired several artists from the shah's ateliers who returned with Humayun to India to found the Mogul school of painting. After Shah Tahmasp's death in 1576, the Safawids were critically weakened by several years of unrest until Shah Abbas I (reigned 1587–1629) restored order to the empire. In 1598 he moved the capital from Qazvīn to Isfahan, where it remained until 1722.

Right, Shah Ismail, in a detail from a mid-seventeenth-century wall painting. Below, a coronation ceremony, painted in 1614, from a Persian manuscript, in the tradition of fifteenth-century Iranian painting under the Timurids (descendants of Tamerlane). Below right, a mounted archer, in a Timurid painting.

Left, a hunting scene, from a sixteenth-century Persian manuscript. The rigid figures and stock types are characteristic of Iranian paintings. Immediately below, two Iranian daggers. Their finely crafted blades and handles are enhanced by inlaid floral patterns and arabesques, typical features of late seventeenth- to eighteenth-century Iranian metalwork. Right, a processional scene, from a late sixteenth-century manuscript produced at Shīrāz, in southern Iran.

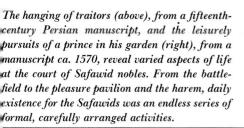

The hanging of traitors (above), from a fifteenth-century Persian manuscript, and the leisurely pursuits of a prince in his garden (right), from a manuscript ca. 1570, reveal varied aspects of life at the court of Safawid nobles. From the battlefield to the pleasure pavilion and the harem, daily existence for the Safawids was an endless series of formal, carefully arranged activities.

Safawid architecture

Above left, a detail of two women and a child from one of the mid-seventeenth-century frescoes in the Chihil Sutun at Isfahan. Below, a view of the great Meidan-i Shah from the balcony of the Ali Kapu. The vast dimensions of the Meidan astonished the many Europeans who visited Shah Abbas I's court and contributed to the European image of the fabulous wealth of the East.

Above, the gilded dome and tiled minarets of the mosque of Fatima, overlooking the central square of Qom. Fatima, the sister of the great spiritual Shi'ite leader Imam Reza, had died at Qom in 816. Years later monuments built to honor important Shi'ites made Qom one of the holiest cities in Iran.

The earliest major Safawid architecture dates from the late sixteenth century when Shah Abbas I extended the city of Isfahan beyond its existing boundaries. The new city developed in a large open space between the city's old walls and the Zayandeh River to the south. The Meidan-i Shah, a great tree-lined tract of land, was at the heart of the complex. At the southern end of the Meidan is the Masjid-i Shah, or Shah's Mosque, completed in 1616. To the north, echoing the mosque's tall, graceful forms, is a gate leading to the bazaars and baths of the commercial section of the city. The palace complex, reached through the Ali Kapu, or high gate (built in the early seventeenth century), is situated to the west. The gate is actually a large pavilion that served as a summer throne room, banquet hall, and review stand. To the west of the gate is the Chihil Sutun (completed by 1647), which literally means pavilion of forty columns, though there are actually only twenty columns reflected in a pool. Opposite the Ali Kapu on the eastern side of the Meidan is the mosque of Shaykh Lutfullah, built between 1598 and 1618. Each of these monuments is rectangular in shape and many have interiors and exteriors covered with elaborately patterned tiles.

Calligraphy was often used to decorate surfaces of Islamic architecture. The intricate designs in ceramic tile on the dome of the Shah's Mosque at Isfahan (above) are an excellent example of the graceful beauty achieved by such decoration. The passages, which are quotations from the Koran, are written in two different kinds of script. Right, a detail from one of the portals of a medrese (school) at Isfahan, built by the last Safawid ruler, Sultan Hussein, in 1710, in honor of his mother. The muqarnas, or small triangular niches, framing the entrance are typical of Islamic architecture. Their complicated patterns are reflected in the geometric tile work of the building's walls.

Right, a seventeenth-century Mogul miniature depicting an audience of a Mogul prince.
Like all Mogul miniatures it is an encyclope-
dia of detail. Each figure's costume is carefully drawn, and his gestures accurately rendered to indicate his rank and mission.
Immediately below, a seventeenth-century
embroidered silk costume. The delicate floral
designs of this coat make it one of the finest
examples of Mogul embroidery. The patterns
for many of these textiles were drawn by the
emperor's master painters.

Below, coins minted by Akbar and Jahangir.
A sign from the zodiac identifies the month in
which the second coin from the left was
minted. The link rings later added to some of
the coins (the last two are opposite sides of the
same coin) enable them to be worn as pen-
dants. Right, Humayun, from a mid-seventeenth-century Mogul miniature.

mystical, growing out of the emperor's conviction that he had achieved certain religious insights that deserved to be shared. In a sense it represented an attempt to create a single spiritual umbrella which would shelter the disparate elements of the empire. Although the religion found few followers, it served to confer upon the emperor an almost divine status. It was, in effect, a personality cult. That it failed is perhaps not so much a fault of the man as an indication of the irreconcilable diversity of his empire.

Artistic developments under Akbar also bore the stamp of his character and interests. He had inherited from his father the services of several Iranian painters whom Humayun, during his exile, had hired away from Shah Tahmasp. As Akbar's sophistication increased, so did that of his painters, whose works the emperor felt rivaled those of contemporary European artists.

Some of the finest and best-known art works produced during Akbar's reign involved the illustration of manuscripts. Ateliers, or workshops, were established in which native artists were trained in the skills of miniature painting and the mixing of colors. When major commissions were ordered, individual pages of a manuscript were assigned to specific artists. Frequently, several artists would work on a single miniature, one man designing the composition, another providing the color, and another doing the portraits, thus facilitating the production of manuscripts that might otherwise have taken decades to paint.

In the earliest of these manuscripts, the *Tuti Nama,* or *Tales of the Parrot,* there is a sense of experimentation, a juxtaposition of the rough, boldly colored drawings of Hindu artists with the more sophisticated designs of Iranian-trained painters. In the *Hamza Nama,* or *Tales of Hamza,* produced slightly later, brilliant designs of palaces and forts combine with powerfully conceived figures and bright colors. During the 1580s and 1590s, paintings became increasingly refined, more delicately colored and conceived. These later manuscripts—of which the *Akbar Nama* (the emperor's memoir) is the outstanding example—reflect Akbar's maturation as a patron.

Akbar supported other areas of the arts as well. His eclectic tastes were reflected in the architecture of his reign, as Hindu and Islamic forms combined to produce a bold and singular style. Though he built monuments at Lahore, Delhi, and Agra, the most significant architectural statement of his reign was the construction of the entire city of Fatehpur Sikri, begun in 1571.

Fatehpur Sikri was built to honor the prophecy of the mystic Shaykh Salim Chisti, who had foreseen the

birth of Akbar's three sons. Composed entirely of red sandstone and conceived in a harmonious style that blends both Moslem and Hindu elements, the complex stands as a microcosm of the world as Akbar saw it. Here imperial grandeur and spiritual awareness paid each other mutual homage. Audience halls were erected for the theological and metaphysical discussions favored by the emperor. One of the most famous of them—the Diwan-i-Khas, or private audience hall—is, in effect, a projection of the emperor's conception of his authority. The hall consists of a single deceptively large chamber with a massive central column connected to elaborately carved balconies by way of four bridges. The emperor would sit atop the column, surrounded by his disputants in the balconies. If they needed to consult the emperor, they would approach by way of a bridge. Below, attendants and observers could watch the proceedings. The building was nothing less than a statement in stone of the hierarchy of Akbar's empire.

Although his concept of an empire was far reaching, Akbar never devised a mechanism for ensuring the peaceful transfer of power from one ruler to the next, thus perpetuating a problem that was to haunt his descendants. While it was often apparent whom an emperor favored as heir, there was no guarantee that his candidate would actually assume the throne.

The possibility always existed that an ambitious claimant might use the death of the reigning emperor as an opportunity to seize the throne for himself.

It was this insecurity over succession that led Akbar's son Salim, later known as Jahangir, to rebel in 1600 and set up his own court at Allahabad, a few hundred miles southeast of Agra (which by 1598 had again become the capital). Born in 1569 to Akbar's Rajput wife Maryam-uz-Zamani, the daughter of the raja of Amber, Salim was the eldest of Akbar's three sons. He seemed destined to succeed his father since his younger brothers were so heavily addicted to opium and alcohol that they were incapable of commanding the large armies entrusted to them. During the 1590s, however, Jahangir, fearing that court intrigues would prevent his succession to the throne, refused to obey orders from his father to undertake military campaigns away from the center of the empire. Although initially only a minor dispute, the rift soon widened to the point where Jahangir fell out of favor with his father.

From 1600 to 1603, Jahangir and his army roamed the country, defying Akbar's orders but never committing any irrevocable acts of treason. (By later standards, this act of filial disloyalty was to seem a relatively polite affair.) After the death of his brothers in 1599 and 1602, father and son were reconciled, but

Far left, Shah Jahan receiving an Iranian embassy in the Diwan-i-Am, or public audience hall, in an eighteenth-century Mogul miniature. He is attended on the left by his sons, and below by several nobles. Formal depictions such as this one are common in seventeenth-century Mogul manuscripts. Artists were charged by their patrons to record every detail of the court so that the emperor could tell exactly who was there at any given time. The peaceful atmosphere of this painting belies the brutal circumstances under which Shah Jahan came to power.

Above, the interior court of the Jahangir Mahal inside the Agra fort. It is believed that this palace was built by Akbar for his son Jahangir. Its richly ornamented walls combine Hindu elements (the pillars and columns at the left) with Moslem forms (the pointed arch and ivans, or recessed cells). This compatible blend of Hindu and Moslem was the guiding principle underlying Akbar's architectural, as well as religious, policies. Right, fort-building activities, from an early seventeenth-century Mogul miniature. The architect in the center is issuing directions to the seemingly confused mass of laborers under his command.

Above, Jahangir embracing his son Shah Jahan, from a seventeenth-century Mogul drawing. Right, Shah Jahan, from a portrait by Balchand, one of the emperor's finest artists. Under Shah Jahan, whose reign was terminated in 1658 when his son Aurangzeb imprisoned him, the Mogul Empire reached its cultural zenith. Artists excelled at painting ever more refined miniatures, and in 1631 construction began on the Taj Mahal. Far right, three lively hunting scenes. Hunting was the Moguls' favorite sport.

only for a short time: Akbar died on October 15, 1605, thereby ending a reign of unparalleled vigor and innovation.

From the strength of his insight, his formidable will, and his understanding, Akbar had created the Mogul Empire out of vastly disparate and hostile elements. His was a rare personal gift. Under Akbar the system of absolute rule went basically unopposed, owing to his grasp of events, his military prowess, and his political acumen. But despite his many reforms, the empire had not progressed beyond that of primarily a military state. As the empire became larger, as its control passed to other, less capable rulers, the system that had been tailored to Akbar's extraordinary abilities would eventually begin to deteriorate.

Jahangir ascended the throne, on October 24, 1605, a very different sort of man from his father. He had grown up in a relatively stable and prosperous court, had received a thorough education in both the arts and sciences, and was something of an aesthete. Unlike his forthright and dynamic father, Jahangir was a man of pronounced extremes. He was capable of such tender-hearted actions as building memorials to favorite animals, yet he could also evince acts of cruelty, as when he ordered the murder of his father's adoring biographer, Abu-l Fazl, in 1602, fearing that this loyal subject might influence his father against him.

The first years of Jahangir's reign were a time of peace and prosperity, marred only by the rebellion of his son Khusrau in 1607. This attempted coup was quickly suppressed and Khusrau imprisoned. The re-

forms established by Akbar continued to function smoothly. Expansion was limited, though later in his reign Jahangir seized territory in the Punjab and made a number of incursions into the Deccan. He wisely adhered to his father's policies of religious tolerance and was rewarded by the continued allegiance of the Rajputs.

Jahangir began his reign with proposals for a number of new reforms in the vein of his father's liberal policies. Excess levies by the *jagadirs,* or holders of jagirs, were forbidden. Merchants' property was not to be forcefully seized and examined on the roads. Property owners were allowed to pass their property

on to their descendants. No less important, the punishment of cutting off ears and noses was forbidden by law.

Despite his early zeal for reform, Jahangir lacked his father's authority when it came to enforcing his programs. As a result, the bureaucracy became increasingly large, complex, and less efficient. Corruption increased and official reserves declined.

In 1611 Jahangir married Mehrunissa, whom he subsequently called Nur Jahan, or Light of the World. This marriage had unexpected political consequences: Both her father, Itimad-ud-Daula, and her brother, Asaf Khan, rose quickly at the court, and the

India's textile trade

From 1600 to 1830, India exported cotton fabrics to almost every market in the civilized world. The extent to which India dominated this trade is reflected even today: "Chintz," "calico," "dungaree," "khaki," and "pajama" are all words of Indian derivation.

The bright colors and fancy designs of Indian textiles appealed to the European taste for exotic, "Oriental" wares during these centuries. It was the price of the fabrics, however, that first attracted the Portuguese, Dutch, and English. As early as 1615, King James of England sent an ambassador, Sir Thomas Roe, to the Mogul court to negotiate favorable trading rights. By the eighteenth century, the Portuguese and Dutch had been superseded by the French as rivals to Britain's East India Company. Competition between the English and the French for this lucrative trade remained intense until 1761, when the English forced the French into submission at the French stronghold of Pondicherry.

Above, a painted cotton textile depicting European figures. This work, with its strong colors and boldly conceived figures, is typical of Madrasi textiles. Below, a seventeenth-century map of the Mogul Empire by Sanson d'Abbeville.

Above, a detail from a sixteenth-century ivory chest depicting a Portuguese sailor and his wife. The carving is remarkable for its intricate design. Note the boar's head on the table and the woman's intricately carved wine cup.

Left, a European sailor, from a late sixteenth-century Mogul miniature. The bold colors, well-modeled features, and subtle characterization of the man's face make this one of the finest Indian studies of a European.

Top right, European sailors shipwrecked off the Indian coast, from a copy of the Akbar Nama. Immediately above, a plate bearing the coat of arms of the French East India Company. Made by the Chinese, this kind of ceramic ware was exported to Europe and the Americas.

Right, the Diwan-i-Khas in the Red Fort at Delhi, built by Shah Jahan in 1648. Inside this audience hall stood the famous Peacock Throne. It remained there until 1739 when the conqueror Nadir Shah sacked Delhi and brought the throne back to Iran. Immediately below, the massive walls of the Red Fort. Although intended to repel enemies, these walls were used by Aurangzeb to imprison his father, Shah Jahan, from 1658 until the Shah's death in 1666. Bottom left, a view from one of the audience halls of the entrance gate to the palatial complex inside the Red Fort.

trio soon wielded considerable influence. During the last years of Jahangir's reign, when he was enfeebled by the same addiction to alcohol and opium that had already killed his brothers, Nur Jahan and her family virtually came to control the empire.

It was during his early years on the throne, a time of political stability, that Jahangir was able to indulge his interest in the arts to an extent that was never possible for his father. In fact it is as a writer and a patron of the arts that Jahangir is chiefly remembered. Jahangir's memoirs abound with exacting descriptions of wild animals, exotic plants, and curiosities. He sometimes even called for animals to be dissected so that he might examine them minutely, and he commissioned his artists to paint unusual animals so that he might pass on to future generations an image as well as a written description.

The emperor's inquisitive mind probed human nature as well. On one memorable occasion, he had a dying courtier carried to him and subjected to the scrutiny of the court artists. Jahangir vividly records the event in his memoirs:

> He appeared so low and weak that I was astonished. He was skin drawn over bones. Or rather his bones, too had dissolved. Though painters have striven much in drawing an emaciated face, yet I have never seen anything like this, nor even approaching it. Good God, can a son of man come to such a shape and fashion. . . . As it was a very extraordinary case I directed painters to take his portrait.

Jahangir's taste in art differed from his father's, a difference that is evident in the specially illustrated copies of the Persian classics on which he directed his artists to work. Bold narrative scenes were now out of favor. The new emperor preferred his artists to explore nuances of form and character. Painting became more subjective. Teamwork was discouraged. As a result illustrations became the individual ex-

Center left, an eighteenth-century painting on silk depicting the audience granted in 1712 to Jan Joshua Ketelaer, trustee of the Dutch East India Company, by Bahadur Shah, Aurangzeb's son and successor. Near left, the Pearl Mosque inside the Red Fort at Delhi. Built by Aurangzeb for his private prayers, the mosque is made entirely of white marble except for the floors, which are inlaid with semiprecious stones. Its walls are decorated with carved floral arabesques. The semiprecious stones and delicate carving give the mosque an almost jewellike quality.

133

Preceding page, the Taj Mahal complex built at Agra by Shah Jahan in memory of his favorite wife, Mumtaz Mahall, who died suddenly in 1631 while giving birth to her fourteenth child. The graceful proportions and exquisite decoration of her tomb, which rests in a splendid garden, are thought to reflect the perfection of Shah Jahan's love for his wife. A large marble waterway leads from the entrance gate to the plinth on which the white marble tomb sits. Inside, an intricately carved marble screen and inlaid floral designs surround the cenotaphs of Shah Jahan and his wife.

pression of a single painter. European techniques of modeling were taken up, because they enabled the artist to better distinguish individual traits; and with this development came a new concern for a sense of space and depth. In response to Jahangir's desire for meticulously rendered studies of individual forms, artists developed a straightforward naturalistic approach that allowed them to create visual equivalents of the emperor's written descriptions.

Jahangir was also capable of turning his powers of observation and description upon himself. His memoir, the *Jahangir Nama,* is full of detailed self-analyses. He reveals himself as both an emperor and a man,

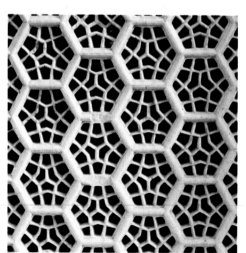

with a frankness that would have shocked his father's biographer Abu-l Fazl. He was surprisingly candid, for example, about his addiction to opium and alcohol. In one extraordinary drawing Jahangir is seen holding a wine cup, his eyes drooping, his skin flaccid. One hand feebly grips the pommel of his sword; the other raises the cup to his lips. It is the portrait of a man striving to maintain his dignity and control against a terrible affliction. In this one revelatory moment, the imperial image is cast aside, revealing the emperor in a moment of extreme vulnerability.

Jahangir was unable to overcome his addiction. As he grew weaker, he was forced to delegate more and more of his official duties to his wife and his in-laws. When the queen's father died in 1622, Jahangir bestowed on Nur Jahan all of his holdings, including his government position: During the last five years of Jahangir's reign, she became, in effect, the most important political figure at court, next to the emperor himself.

Left, the tomb of Itimad-ud-Daula, Jahangir's father-in-law, built by Nur Jahan (Jahangir's wife) in 1628. The structure, whose finely inlaid walls anticipate those of the Taj Mahal, is situated across the river and downstream from the Taj. Below left, three tomb details, revealing the intricacy of the ornamentation. Right, the Jahangir Mahal inside the Red Fort at Agra. Although begun by Akbar, additions to the fort continued through the reign of Shah Jahan. Below, a view of the fort's seventy-foot-high walls.

Throughout Jahangir's declining years tensions between Nur Jahan and Jahangir's son Khurram, better known as Shah Jahan, intensified as each struggled for dominance in selecting an heir to the throne. In 1620 Jahangir ordered Shah Jahan to the Deccan to suppress the guerrilla activities of his rivals there. Shah Jahan was reluctant to go, since he realized that the Mogul army was ill-equipped to combat such tactics. Moreover he feared that a setback in the Deccan would disgrace him and give Nur Jahan a superior position in any future negotiations over succession. He finally set off for the south in 1621 and was able to negotiate a treaty with the dissidents.

The Portuguese

In 1487, forty years before Baber's victory at the battle of Panipat, the Portuguese sailor Pedro de Covilhão reached the west coast of India. Eleven years later he was followed by Vasco da Gama, and by the first decade of the sixteenth century, the Portuguese were firmly entrenched on India's western shore. Seeking initially to engage in the lucrative spice trade, the Portuguese soon became heavily involved in exporting textiles back to European markets.

Among the many items the Portuguese brought to India were illustrated manuscripts and bibles, some of which reached the Mogul court during the 1570s. Akbar was so intrigued by this vast assortment of riches that in 1579 he sent an envoy to the Portuguese authorities in Goa requesting representatives of their religion. In response, a year later a mission of three Jesuit priests arrived at Akbar's court at Fatehpur Sikri.

Many of the Portuguese who came to India wrote detailed accounts of their experiences. They were particularly amazed by the strange dress and customs of the Hindus as well as by the wealth and grandeur of the Mogul court. Their exotic descriptions of Indian life found a ready audience in Europe; books such as João de Barros' *History of the Portuguese Conquests Overseas* became standard texts in fashionable libraries.

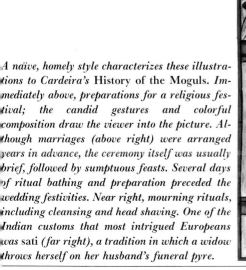

A naïve, homely style characterizes these illustrations to Cardeira's History of the Moguls. Immediately above, preparations for a religious festival; the candid gestures and colorful composition draw the viewer into the picture. Although marriages (above right) were arranged years in advance, the ceremony itself was usually brief, followed by sumptuous feasts. Several days of ritual bathing and preparation preceded the wedding festivities. Near right, mourning rituals, including cleansing and head shaving. One of the Indian customs that most intrigued Europeans was sati (far right), a tradition in which a widow throws herself on her husband's funeral pyre.

Golconda was one of the richest Moslem sultanates of the Deccan. Although it withstood many Mogul attacks throughout the late sixteenth and early seventeenth centuries, in 1687, after a seven-and-one-half-month siege by Aurangzeb, the ancient city finally fell to the invaders. Golconda's success at resisting the Moguls can be attributed partly to its mighty fortress (above, two views). With walls of granite, seventy-six bastions standing sixty feet high, and gates studded with iron spikes, this fortress proved a formidable barrier to warriors and elephants alike.

Right, Dara Shikoh, Shah Jahan's favorite son, from an eighteenth-century Mogul miniature. An intellectual like his great-grandfather Akbar, he wrote long essays on the relationship between Hinduism and Islam. His heterodox tendencies infuriated his brother Aurangzeb, who, backed by many of the court nobles, usurped the throne from his father in 1658. Supported by the army, Dara Shikoh met Aurangzeb in a fierce battle only to lose the fight when he dismounted his elephant, inadvertently giving his army the sign of defeat.

Despite this victory, his insecurity was still evident: He had his brother Khusrau, a prisoner at Jahangir's court, murdered, fearing that he might be a potential rival for the throne. In 1622 he entered into open rebellion against his father. The immediate provocation for the revolt was Jahangir's order to Shah Jahan to march his army northwest from the Deccan to protect Kandahār from imminent attack. Shah Jahan suspected that the marching orders were a scheme of Nur Jahan's to keep him at a distance, away from any potential base of support. His fears, in fact, may have been justified, for Nur Jahan had become the champion of a younger prince, Shahriyar, to whom several of Shah Jahan's jagirs were being transferred.

Shah Jahan refused to march. For the next three years he was constantly on the move, trying to avoid the imperial army that Jahangir had sent out after him. Finally, in 1625, he sued for peace and was granted lenient terms: the surrender of two fortresses and two of his sons to Jahangir's court as hostages. During the next two years, there were constant battles for power. Amid the unrest, the general Mahabat Khan rebelled, capturing the ailing emperor, his wife, and several nobles and briefly holding them prisoner. Jahangir finally died, in the Punjab, in the fall of 1627. In the ensuing battle over succession to the throne, Shah Jahan allied himself with Nur Jahan's brother, Asaf Khan, against the queen's interests. Asaf Khan proved extremely adept at manipulating plays for power, confining his sister to the harem, rescuing Shah Jahan's two sons from her care, and forcing her protégé, Shahriyar, to fight, although backed by a weak and inexperienced army. Eventually Shah Jahan was able to claim the throne for himself. Yet it was a prize that had exacted a price. He had been responsible for the murder of one of his brothers, two nephews, and two cousins—a bloody prelude to the events to come.

Women in Mogul India

Bedecked in jewels and smelling of sweet perfume, the women of the Mogul court were an awesome presence, chosen for both their beauty and intelligence. Although forbidden to be seen outside the harem—their private living quarters—these princesses exerted considerable influence because of their accessibility to the emperor. Their counsel was frequently solicited by nobles and visitors to the court, who were permitted to approach the harem by the court eunuchs.

Members of the harem could observe court functions through screened partitions, often discreetly interceding on behalf of a favorite caller. Their judgments were not to be overlooked, as one word from a ranking princess could either condemn or acquit a subject.

At times women even took control of the government, while remaining, of course, in purdah (screened from the sight of men). Such was the case of Nur Jahan, Jahangir's favorite wife. Guarded by her eunuchs and protected by a screen, she ruled the empire during the last years of the emperor's life when he was unable to deal with the tedium of day-to-day functions. If the court went hunting so did she, shooting tigers from an enclosed carriage. In 1625 Nur Jahan even rode into battle in a covered litter supported by two elephants.

Above, a polo match, from an eighteenth-century Mogul miniature. Polo, which came to the West from China, was a sport in which Mogul women sometimes participated.

Below left, a Mogul princess, from a miniature of the late seventeenth to early eighteenth century. Although outsiders were generally permitted only fleeting glimpses of the women of the harem, exceptions seem to have been made for the artists who painted their portraits. Immediately below, a ruler and his consort, from an eighteenth-century Rajput miniature.

Women play an intrinsic role in Indian art, appearing in both secular and sacred roles. One of the standard ideals of female beauty is epitomized in the character of Draupadi, the heroine of the Mahābhārata *(one of the great Indian epics). Her attributes include long black curly hair, eyes shaped like a leaf from a lotus blossom, a slim waist, a red mouth, shapely hips, and firm thighs. During the eighteenth and nineteenth centuries, when the Rajput courts of northwest India and the Punjab hills began to supersede the Mogul court as the artistic center of India, Mogul notions of portraiture combined with Indian ideals of beauty. The results were striking. In a painting from the Punjab (ca. 1700) of a prince and two attendants (top right), women are seen as ideal consorts. A somewhat later eighteenth-century painting (immediately above), also from the Punjab, depicts a princess writing. Right, an eighteenth-century painting from the Deccan showing a prince wooing one of the court beauties.*

143

Shah Jahan's reign is remembered primarily as a time of major artistic achievement. It was the age of the Taj Mahal, the Peacock Throne, and the Red Fort at Delhi. The appearance of tranquility and sumptuous elegance, however, hid deeply rooted political dissatisfactions. The liberal policies of religious and social tolerance of the late sixteenth and early seventeenth centuries were gradually being supplanted by a growing conservatism and rigidity. By the 1640s and 1650s, the empire had also begun to suffer a series of military setbacks, the greatest of which was the permanent loss of Kandahār—one of the most important commercial crossroads in Asia—to the Iranians in 1649.

Kandahār had been the scene of intense conflict between the Moguls and the Iranians during the 1620s, when Shah Abbas I took the town from Jahangir. In 1638, it was returned to the Moguls when the Iranian governor of the city, Ali Mardan Khan, switched allegiance and surrendered the town. Ten years later, Shah Abbas II sent a large army to retake

Kandahār, and before Mogul reinforcements, under the command of Shah Jahan's son Aurangzeb, could arrive, the town had fallen. Despite two more massive and costly attempts to regain the town—one by Aurangzeb in 1652, the other by his elder brother, Dara Shikoh, in 1653—Kandahār remained in the hands of the Iranians.

The Deccan also continued to plague the Moguls, despite several treaties acknowledging Mogul sovereignty in the area. In 1635, Shah Jahan and Aurangzeb marched south into the Deccan in a show of strength and Aurangzeb was appointed as his father's representative there. He proved extremely able—using military force when necessary, administering the land well, and maintaining control of the region—but was summarily relieved of his post in 1644 owing to court intrigues. Several years later, when the troublesome Deccani kingdoms of Bijapur and Golconda began to assert their independence, Aurangzeb returned to the Deccan to restore peace—through negotiation rather than battle. As a result the kingdoms

Left, the fortified city of Jodhpur, a former capital of the district of Marwar in Rajasthan. Built in 1459 by Marharaja Rao Jodha, the city stands on a low sandstone hill and is surrounded by an immense wall having a periphery of six miles. Above, Malasri Ragini, from a seventeenth-century Rajput miniature. Right, Todi Ragini, from a Rajput miniature ca. 1680. Raginis, the wives of Ragas, are the subject of a series of illustrations known as Ragmalas, which were extremely popular at the Rajput courts. Both ragas and raginis were personifications of musical modes.

Left, a prince and his consorts listening to musicians, from a late seventeenth- or eighteenth-century Ragmala. Ragmala illustrations represent visual interpretations of Indian forms of music. Their subject matter is usually romantic and is often set in aristocratic surroundings. Following pages, the walled city of Amber, home of an influential Rajput family. In 1562 Akbar married into one of the most powerful Rajput families, securing its loyalty to his empire.

Left, a detail of the Chandir Mandir, or Moon Palace, at Jaipur. Above, the upper stories of the Hall of Winds, one of Jaipur's most famous palaces, built in the 1760s. Below, the Peacock Gate, an entrance to the Ladies' Court at Jaipur.

retained their armies and thus their means of thwarting Mogul efforts in the region.

These uprisings gave warning that the empire was no longer strong enough to pursue expansion. Meanwhile, no new funds were coming in to replenish the imperial treasury, which was rapidly depleted by expensive building programs and costly military campaigns. In an effort to improve his dismal financial situation, Shah Jahan permitted his nobles to increase the amount of tax they collected from their jagirs, encouraging many peasants to conceal their wealth and decrease productivity to avoid being taxed exorbitantly. Such ill-advised tactics led the empire to the verge of economic stagnation.

A similar lack of vitality was afflicting the arts. Although numerous monuments were built during Shah Jahan's reign—such as the enormous Red Fort at Delhi, with its white marble pavilions, elaborate gardens, and intricate watercourses—Mogul architecture had reached its zenith. The innovation and vigor of earlier buildings had vanished, leaving in its place a static perfection. This sort of passive beauty is most readily seen in the Taj Mahal, the most famous of all Mogul monuments.

In 1631 Mumtaz Mahall, Shah Jahan's favorite wife, died giving birth to her fourteenth child. Shortly thereafter construction began on her tomb, the Taj

Maharaja Jai Singh II, who founded the north Indian city of Jaipur in 1728, was an avid astronomer. Within his new city he built a giant observatory known as the Yantar Mantar. By enlarging the size of normal astronomical devices, the maharaja hoped to improve their accuracy. However, in the case of the Samrai Yantar (above), whose gnomon (an object that projects a shadow) is ninety feet, the theory failed: The structure is so large that its shadow is too blurred to be accurately read. Jai Singh also built a similar, though structurally simpler, observatory in Delhi.

Mahal, at Agra. Perhaps because of the purity of form and balance and the peacefulness of the surroundings, sentimentalists have always assumed that the Taj is a testimony to Shah Jahan's love of his wife and his lasting faithfulness to her memory. This notion, however, has been received with some cynicism by those who believe accounts indicating that Shah Jahan may have carried on an incestuous relationship with one of his daughters for many years following Mumtaz Mahall's death. Whatever his motivation in building the tomb, Shah Jahan's monument has often been compared to a jewel—perfectly balanced, each section complementing the next.

The main buildings were most likely finished within four years, though it took another twenty to complete the entire complex. Standing over two hundred and fifty feet tall at its highest point, the Taj, a white marble octagon, sits in a garden divided into four parts by formal watercourses. The queen's tomb rests on a large rectangular plinth, or platform, also made of marble. At each corner of the plinth is a white marble minaret. A large onion dome crowns the tomb. Inside, the walls, punctuated by arched openings, are inlaid with floral designs set with semi-precious stones.

In approaching the Taj, one walks toward the plinth along a straight pathway that then turns away from the tomb toward a flight of stairs running parallel to the monument. This indirect approach, forcing the visitor to circulate around the base of the plinth, subtly manipulates one's perceptions of the structure: The Taj was intended to be admired from all perspectives, exactly as an observer would perceive a precious sculptural work. In the sophistication and clarity of its design, as well as its formal white exterior, the Taj Mahal emanates an almost self-conscious beauty. With the Taj Mahal, the enthusiasm, creativity, and innovative spirit that characterized earlier periods in Mogul architecture gave way to sheer technical perfection.

This emphasis on technical virtuosity also extended to the paintings sponsored during Shah Jahan's reign. Under his patronage, painters excelled at technical execution and were encouraged to portray the emperor in ever more formal and stately poses. Techniques of modeling and space eventually came to be regarded as ends in themselves, with the result that

With the death in 1712 of Bahadur Shah, Aurangzeb's successor, the Mogul Empire lost much of its stability. In 1719 alone, four puppet kings ascended the Mogul throne. One of them, Farruk-Siar (left), has been immortalized in an early eighteenth-century Mogul miniature. The attention lavished on the king's jewels and fine clothing suggests the superficiality of his reign.

compositions often seemed to lack the spontaneity and naturalism that typified art under the patronage of Jahangir.

There are, in fact, obvious connections between Shah Jahan's preferences in art and his temperament. One of our most revealing assessments of the ruler as a young prince is found in the expansive memoirs of Sir Thomas Roe, King James' ambassador to the Mogul court from 1615 to 1619. He does not attempt to disguise his feelings about the future shah: "I never saw so settled a countenance, nor any man keep so constant a gravity, nor in face showing any respect or difference of men; but mingled with extreme pride and contempt for all." In this undiplomatic vein, Sir Thomas captures a sense of Jahan's formality and reserve, tendencies that were reflected in his ostentatious taste as patron.

The Peacock Throne, commissioned upon Shah Jahan's accession and finished in 1634, was a fitting symbol of the emperor and his empire. Although the throne was seized by Iranian troops during the sack of Delhi in 1739 and subsequently broken apart, several descriptions of it have survived. One of the most detailed is from the memoirs of the French jeweler Jean Baptiste Tavernier, written ca. 1665:

The principal throne . . . resembles in form and size our camp beds; that is to say, it is about six feet long and four wide. Upon the four feet, which are very massive . . . are fixed the four bars which support the base of the throne, and upon these bars are ranged twelve columns, which sustain the canopy. . . . Above the canopy which is a quadrangular shaped dome there is a peacock with elevated tail made of blue sapphires and other colored stones, the body of gold inlaid with precious stones,

Above, Rama and Sita, in an example of early eighteenth-century Pahari painting, which developed in the Punjab hills. Rama was the seventh incarnation of the Hindu god Vishnu, and Sita his devoted wife. Right, a detail from an eighteenth-century Deccani miniature. The deer is a symbol of love in Hindu mythology, frequently signifying a woman's yearning for her absent lord.

Shah Alam (above left) grants Robert Clive of the British East India Company the right to collect taxes in Bengal, Bihar, and Orissa in this painting by Benjamin West. Shah Alam's action in 1765 effectively gave Britain authority over these provinces, capping several years of military victories by the British, who had begun military operations in India after the nawab, or governor, of Bengal attacked their garrison at Calcutta in 1756. Left, an officer of the British East India Company smoking a hookah, or water pipe, from a Mogul miniature ca. 1760.

having a large ruby in front of the breast, whence hangs a pear-shaped pearl of fifty carats.

Like the throne with its precious jewels, Shah Jahan's reign appeared on the surface to be opulent and splendid. Yet his influence on the empire was predominantly negative, and sometimes even destructive. In ignoring or rejecting the eclectic tastes and policies of his predecessors, Shah Jahan embraced the rigidity and conservatism that were to precipitate the collapse of Mogul rule in India.

Unlike his father and grandfather, Shah Jahan was not committed to religious tolerance. Before long, tensions between Hindus and Moslems were increasing. In 1632 the emperor ordered the destruction of all new Hindu temples, a shocking regression to policies that had long since been abandoned.

Shah Jahan's own attitude toward the Hindus, however, is difficult to fathom, for he continued to patronize Hindu poets, musicians, and artists. Perhaps his inflexible policy on religious Orthodoxy did not extend to giving up the luxuries afforded by the policy it had replaced. The ambiguities evident in his conduct make it impossible to ascertain whether his actions were self-determined or were a response to mounting pressure from the Orthodox elements at court. Whatever their cause the effect was to strengthen these conservative factions to the extent that the Orthodox ulema once again began to acquire a major role at court. With this reversion to theocracy came a growing tendency toward conservatism in all spheres of life.

The tension between the new Orthodox attitudes at court and the still-circulating liberal ideas of Akbar and Jahangir reached a climax in the conflict between Dara Shikoh, Shah Jahan's eldest son, and Aurangzeb. Dara, like his great-grandfather Akbar, was intensely interested in theological issues and shared many of Akbar's universalist beliefs. He frequented numerous Hindu and Moslem holy men, most notably Mian Mir, a Sufi mystic. On several occasions, Dara even claimed to have had mystical experiences, as had Akbar before him.

Although uninterested in historical studies and issues of Islamic jurisprudence, Dara was fascinated by the relationship between Hindu and Islamic mysticism. He translated a number of Hindu texts, such as the *Bhagavad-Gita*, from Hindustani into Persian and wrote a number of treatises, including a hagio-

Yoga

Among the marvels of India that capti-
vated the attention of Europeans in the
East were the ascetic exercises of the yogi.
Based on an austere view of life, yoga sets
out to overcome physical sensibilities by
controlling the movements of the body.
Through a series of breathing and body
exercises the yogi strives to disassociate his
soul from his body until it is free to fuse
with God. In the process the yogi learns to
transcend many physical sensations, including pain. It was this ability to master
pain—demonstrated by such feats as walk-
ing on nails or fire—rather than the philo-
sophic basis of yoga that proved most
compelling to Europeans in India.

*Left, two Indians praying to a Hindu
holy man, from an illustration to Cardeira's eighteenth-century* History of
the Moguls. *The holy man, isolated in
his ascetic dwelling, is seated in a yoga
position known as the lotus and is accompanied by a disciple.*

Clockwise from upper left, five yoga positions from Cardeira's History of the Moguls: the kukkutasana, or cock, a variant of the lotus position; the utkatasana, or seat; the vrishjasansa, or scorpion; the vatyanasana, or half-leg; and the sirshasana, or upside-down position. The remarkable detail of these illustrations hints at the appeal yoga must have had for Europeans living in India during the eighteenth century.

Left, three scenes of the battle of Pollilur (1780), from the Daria Daulat pavilion in Seringapatam. Under the command of General Baillie (center, in the palanquin, or covered conveyance), the British were soundly defeated by Tipu Sultan and his allies. The ruler of Mysore, Tipu Sultan fought against the British, until he was defeated and killed by them. Right, a portrait of Tipu Sultan by G.F. Cherry.

graphy of Moslem saints and a lengthy tract comparing Hinduism to Islam.

The liberal attitudes of Dara were firmly opposed by his brother Aurangzeb, whose intellectual interests were devoted strictly to Orthodox Moslem thought. Aurangzeb took an avid interest in Islamic law, and it was to him that the Orthodox elements at court gravitated—rather than to Dara, whose heterodoxy represented a dangerous threat.

By 1644 the tension between the two brothers had become overt. Aurangzeb violently objected to Dara's role as favorite son, and his constant complaints to Shah Jahan about Dara's religious attitudes may have figured largely in the emperor's decision to remove Aurangzeb from his command in the Deccan. Ironically, by favoring Dara, Shah Jahan was depriving him of the military and political experience

The English fought three campaigns against Tipu Sultan. In the first, the battle of Pollilur, they were routed. The second campaign, which included the siege of Bangalore (March 8, 1792), was won by the British forces, although they suffered great losses such as the death of General Moorhouse (above). Despite his defeat, Tipu Sultan refused to disarm, perhaps because he believed that Napoleon would come to his aid. Instead, the British, under the command of General Cornwallis (left), besieged and killed the sultan at Seringapatam in 1799.

gained by his younger brother, who was being moved about the country from one post to another. Perhaps Shah Jahan simply feared that a more military-minded Dara might rebel against him as the emperor had rebelled against his own father, Jahangir. Whatever his reason, he kept Dara with him at court as his heir apparent, while the resentful Aurangzeb was in distant regions, quietly gaining military expertise and a following of loyal soldiers.

Aurangzeb's defeats by the Iranians at Kandahār in 1649 and again in 1652 were seen as major setbacks in his career, even though Dara, marching on Kandahār in 1653 with an even larger army, also met with failure. Throughout his reign, Shah Jahan remained steadfast in his preference for Dara, further alienating Aurangzeb and his faction.

Antagonisms between the brothers surfaced in 1657, when Shah Jahan became ill at Delhi. Once it appeared that the emperor might die, all three of Dara's younger brothers—Shah Shuja, Aurangzeb, and Murad Baksh—began maneuvering to march on Delhi to claim the throne. Aurangzeb, however, let Shah Shuja and Murad Baksh make the opening moves. In a series of minor battles, Dara's forces, consisting of the imperial army under the command of Dara's eldest son, Suleiman Shikoh, defeated the forces of Shah Shuja near Benares (Varanasi). However in April of 1658, Dara's secondary forces, led by the Rajput Jaswant Singh, were badly defeated by Aurangzeb at Dharmat. Aurangzeb now marched north toward Delhi, while Dara prepared to meet him with his remaining troops.

The two armies met on May 29 at Samugarh, near Agra. In a furious battle fought on elephant and on

Left, a maharaja hunting boar, from an early nineteenth-century Rajput miniature. Boar hunting, which could be very dangerous, was one of the Rajputs' favorite types of hunting. In Mewar, where this miniature was painted, boars were kept in a special park. Each spring, during a festival in honor of the goddess Gauri, the nobles of the state would partake in an enormous boar hunt.

Right, a mid-nineteenth-century portrait of Lord Ellenborough. Appointed governor general of India in 1841, Lord Ellenborough was directed to restore peace in India after the turbulent years of Lord Auckland's governor generalship. Unable to do so, he was recalled to England in 1844.

foot, the combined contingents of Aurangzeb, Murad Baksh, and Shah Shuja defeated the forces of the much less experienced Dara. Barely escaping with his life, Dara fled to Sind, while Aurangzeb marched on Agra. There, Shah Jahan, who had recovered from his illness, received him. In an effort to appease Aurangzeb and acknowledge his victory at Samugarh, he presented his son with a special sword, known as Alamgir, or World Seizer, a title Aurangzeb subsequently adopted. When Aurangzeb demanded that the fort at Agra be turned over to him, however, Shah Jahan refused. Furious, Aurangzeb set siege to the city. His cause was advanced by the lack of fresh drinking water, and within days the emperor capitulated. With the fall of the fort and his victory over the imperial army, Aurangzeb's coup d'état was virtually complete. Shah Jahan, imprisoned inside the Red Fort at Agra, remained there until his death in 1666, a broken and desolate man.

Aurangzeb's remaining preoccupation was the fear that Dara and his two brothers would regain power. Within a year, Dara had been taken prisoner, and on August 30, 1659, he was executed on charges of heresy. The French traveler François Bernier offers a last glimpse of the defeated prince:

> seated on a miserable and worn-out animal, covered with filth; he no longer wore the necklace of large pearls which distinguish the princes of Hindustan, nor the rich turban and embroidered coat; he and his son [Siphor Shikoh] were now habited in dirty cloth of the coarsest texture, and his sorry turban was wrapped round with a Kashmir shawl or scarf, resembling that worn by the meanest people.

Prince Murad Baksh was imprisoned that same year and murdered on December 4, 1661, at Aurangzeb's order. The remaining brother, Shah Shuja, fled the country in 1663. Continuing the carnage, Aurangzeb also ordered the execution of his nephew Suleiman Shikoh, who had been captured in the Punjab, and

Near left, a pastoral scene, from a Pahari miniature ca. 1780. In the lower left foreground are cowherds accompanied by Krishna. To the right are a number of villagers in their houses. The careful detail and lively expressions on the figures' faces create a sense of village life in late eighteenth- to early nineteenth-century India. Unlike the major cities of India and certain parts of Rajasthan, the remote hills of the Punjab remained largely untouched by the British during the late eighteenth and early nineteenth centuries.

Animals in Mogul miniatures

The Moguls were extremely sensitive to their environment. The memoirs of Baber, Akbar, and Jahangir abound with observations on the wildlife of India. The late sixteenth- and seventeenth-century artists who illustrated these manuscripts were equally concerned with nature. By copying European prints circulating at the Mogul court they learned the techniques of modeling and foreshortening, enabling them to infuse their work with a sense of life and character, as well as detail.

Under Jahangir, artists developed even finer means of portraying the detail that interested the emperor. One artist, Mansur, was so skilled at rendering animals, that he was given the title "Wonder of the Age" by Jahangir. By the eighteenth century this taste for natural history had reached several Rajput courts. However, whereas the Moguls favored detail, the Rajputs preferred generalized types, creating metaphorical images instead of realistic portraits.

Right, a detail of a tiger hunt, from a late eighteenth-century Kotah (a district in Rajasthan) miniature. The eerie light and stunted trees are a fittingly electrifying backdrop. The almost allegorical qualities of this painting contrast with the carefully rendered studies (below, left and right) of two gazelles, from a late sixteenth-century Mogul miniature.

Top left, a zebra, from a miniature painting by Mansur, ca. 1620. Mansur was noted for his ability to produce almost microscopically accurate renderings of animals and plants. He accomplished this in the picture of the zebra by isolating his figure against a relatively neutral background and then depicting every hair of the animal's skin. He often used different types of strokes to capture the various textures of his subject's form. Immediately above and right, two scenes from fifteenth- and early sixteenth-century copies of The Fables of Bidpai.

Above, a detail of a bird and a butterfly, from a mid-seventeenth-century Iranian miniature. Natural history paintings, especially bird and flower studies, became extremely popular at the Safawid court in Iran during the seventeenth and eighteenth centuries. Like Mogul miniatures, these studies tend to isolate a single figure against a simple background. Yet because they rely so heavily on European effects of modeling and perspective, they lack the sympathetic understanding of the subject's character found in Mogul art.

Above, the battle of Nagpur (December 16, 1817), from a nineteenth-century painting. The British victory over the Marathas in this struggle gave them control over most of central India. Below, Bahadur Shah II, the last Mogul emperor, from a nineteenth-century Mogul miniature. Below right, a painting depicting the battle of Chialianwala (January 13, 1849), which ended in a British victory over the Sikhs.

Suleiman's two sons, sparing only the life of Dara's young son Siphor Shikoh, whom he held prisoner until 1673.

Aurangzeb's fratricidal victory represented the triumph of Orthodoxy at the Mogul court. Soon he was unraveling the fragile religious alliance that had held the empire together. In 1668 the emperor prohibited the writing of official court histories on the grounds that such actions constituted human worship and verged on idolatry, thus violating the strict monotheistic basis of Islam. He prohibited music and alcohol at the court and took up his father's previously unsuccessful policy of destroying recently built Hindu temples, as well as prohibiting the construction of new ones. The most damaging of Aurangzeb's decrees was the reinstitution of the jizya, once again taxing all nonbelievers, and thus ending over a century of religious tolerance.

Economically the country was also in a decline. Determined to conquer the Deccan once and for all, Aurangzeb marched south in 1681 on a campaign that was to last the rest of his life and bring the empire to the verge of bankruptcy. At first success came relatively quickly. In 1686 Bijapur fell, followed by Golconda in 1687. Their kings were imprisoned,

Above, the Khyber Pass, between present-day Pakistan and Afghanistan. Throughout the mid-nineteenth century this vital mountain pass was the scene of many ambushes between the British and the Afghans.

and the area came under the control of the Moguls. But Aurangzeb was not content to stop there. He hoped to subdue all the remaining forts and minor kingdoms of the region as well. Under the best of circumstances this was a grueling task, because it meant fighting indigenous troops in dry, hostile territory. For the large Mogul army it was disastrous. They were forced to fight small bands of Maratha tribesmen who knew the area well. This mobile group of hill people, before 1680 under the brilliant military leadership of a guerrilla fighter named Shivaji and now under the command of his son Shambhuji, struck quietly at the virtually immobile Mogul army. Although never inflicting heavy losses, their relentless attacks successfully hindered the Mogul forces, which at one point numbered over one hundred and fifty thousand fighting troops. Each time the Moguls captured a fort and moved on, the Marathas simply returned and reoccupied it, demoralizing the Mogul army and forcing the Moguls to scatter their forces across the entire region. The Moguls were spending vast sums of money on this hopeless endeavor, and the troops soon faced starvation on land they themselves had devastated.

The arts were to fare even worse under Aurangzeb than did the army and the economy. During the early years of his reign, painters were still at work illustrating manuscripts, and major architectural projects were in progress. Perhaps the most successful of these is the Pearl Mosque (Moti Masjid) within the Red Fort at Delhi, completed in 1659. Built entirely of white marble, this small but superbly decorated building is one of the most beautiful of all Mogul mosques. Its walls are composed of large floral and geometric reliefs and its floors of inlaid floral designs which lend the building a warmth its otherwise austere white surfaces lack.

Despite the construction of this and other buildings, patronage of the arts soon dwindled at the

In 1857 the sepoys, or native soldiers (left), in the British army revolted, beginning a two-year mutiny that left the British with complete control of India. The immediate provocation of the revolt was a rumor that the East India Company had given the sepoys ammunition coated with the fat of cows (sacred to Hindus) and of pigs (detested by Moslems). From its source in Berhampore, the rebellion quickly spread to Lucknow, Delhi, and Cawnpore (Kanpur), where the entire British colony was massacred. By April 1859, however, the British reconquest was complete, though rule of India was transferred from the East India Company to the crown. Below, Charles John Canning, governor of India during the rebellion and, later, first viceroy of India.

Mogul court. Unlike his predecessors Aurangzeb was not interested in the Persian and Hindu literary works that had kept calligraphers and illustrators occupied throughout the first half of the seventeenth century. Musicians, painters, and poets began seeking patronage elsewhere, especially after the 1680s, by which time the Deccan campaigns had drained the imperial treasury of all available funds. By severing the link with Hindu India from which the Moguls had drawn so much of their strength and inspiration,

and by committing himself to a lengthy, unproductive war in the south, Aurangzeb effectively ended imperial patronage of the arts at the Mogul court.

Aurangzeb lived until 1707. He had seen the fortunes of the empire descend from the heyday of Jahangir and had been largely responsible for its diminished state. His descendants were even less fortunate. Over the next thirty-two years, a succession of ten emperors ruled a greatly reduced realm until 1739, when the Afghan conqueror Nadir Shah sacked

Above, the so-called "slaughter house" at Cawnpore where the British were massacred by the rebel army of Nana Sahib. The rebellion's early success came as a great surprise to the British, who were unaware of their strained relations with the native population. In particular, they had antagonized the wealthy Indian and Mogul princes with the threat of land reforms and confiscations. Because of this, the latter initially supported the rebels, allowing them to spread their mutiny throughout India. Left, the water station at Barwarie, the site of one of the British army's most heroic defenses.

Delhi was one of the first cities to fall to the rebels during the Indian Mutiny. Britain's attempt to regain the capital (September 14–20, 1857) produced a fierce battle in which the English troops, under the command of General Nicholson, rushed the walls of the city in a number of wild charges. One such assault, at the Gate of Kashmir (below), led to a furious struggle eventually won by the British. They ultimately recovered the entire city, and immediately after the end of the rebellion carried out a number of executions (right) before a general clemency was granted to the population.

Delhi. Although he did not remain to rule the country, he made off with much of what was left of the imperial treasuries, including the famed Peacock Throne. From then until their final demise in 1858, the Mogul emperors were reduced to puppets, while an almost endless series of political factions sought to gain control of the country. The most important of these were the French and English, who had come to India during the seventeenth century to profit from the lucrative cotton and spice trade.

Initially the presence of the British and French in India was limited to privately owned commercial ventures that hinged upon friendly relations with the Moguls. With the dissolution of Mogul power during the eighteenth century, however, these enterprises— the British and French East India companies—found themselves in control of large areas: the French of the southeastern coastal cities of Madras and Pondicherry; the British of Bombay to the west and Calcutta to the east. The companies now had territorial as well as commercial interests in India, and an in-

creased rivalry subsequently developed between the two as each tried to enlarge its holdings. The stakes were considerable, for yearly profits of several million dollars were common, and the market was expanding in Europe and North America.

The inevitable clash between the British and French companies finally occurred during the 1740s and 1750s, sparked not only by events in India but also by wars in Europe: As the French and English found themselves on opposing sides in the War of Austrian Succession (1742) and later in the Seven Years' War (1756–1763), a general climate of hostility developed that helped fuel the existing rivalry in India. The French took the first initiative, seizing Madras from the British in 1746. For the next fifteen years, the two countries engaged in a number of minor skirmishes in and around Madras and Pondicherry; these ended when the English defeated the French at the southeastern town of Wandiwash in 1760 and at Pondicherry in 1761.

During the time that the British were battling the

French in the south, they also were involved in a fight with Siraj-ud-Daula, the nawab, or governor, of Bengal. Bengal had become independent of the Mogul Empire several years earlier. On June 20, 1756, Siraj attacked Calcutta, imprisoning one hundred and forty-five men and one woman for a night in the Black Hole, or jail, of Fort William. The heat was stifling, and when the door was opened the next morning, almost all of the prisoners were dead. The British were naturally horrified by this incident, and Robert Clive of the East India Company was dispatched to settle the affair. Although a treaty was signed on February 9, 1757, restoring company privileges, Clive was not content to let matters rest: On June 23, he met and defeated Siraj's army at the battle of Plassey.

As a result of its subjugation of the French and its victory in Bengal, the British East India Company now found itself not only in control of trade throughout most of India but in control of the government of Bengal as well. Rather than choosing to rule directly, the British instead sanctioned the continuation of administrative policies established by the Moguls (the revenue collected from taxes, though, now passed to the company's coffers). With these new powers, however, came increased governmental regulations from England. In 1773 British parliament passed the Regulating Act, which allowed it to gain partial control of the company's Indian settlements, and in 1784 passed a second Indian Act which placed the East India Company under the supervision of a Board of Control nominated by the British government.

In the last quarter of the eighteenth century, the East India Company extended its control to the south and west, annexing most of the Moguls' former domains. From 1762 until 1782, British efforts to take over the Deccani kingdom of Mysore were thwarted by the kingdom's powerful ruler, Haider Ali Khan. After his death in 1782, however, his son and successor, Tipu Sultan, fared less successfully. Although he at first gained a number of easy victories against the British, Tipu Sultan was defeated by them in 1784.

Five years later he rose in rebellion; but under the leadership of Lord Cornwallis, the East India Company's army quelled the rebellion in 1792. In 1798, with the hope of forming an alliance with the French, who were campaigning successfully in Egypt, Tipu again rose in rebellion. Unfortunately, the French alliance never materialized, and in 1799 he was attacked and killed by the British at his stronghold in Seringapatam.

To the west, the British had been encroaching upon the lands of the Marathas. At first British efforts were checked by the Marathas' skillful fighting. During the first decades of the nineteenth century, however, the tribesmen were unable to maintain a unified defense. As their power declined, the British, led by Arthur Wellsley, the future duke of Wellington, chased the Marathas from one area to the next, persistently weakening their forces. Although Wellsley was recalled to England in 1805, the British continued to pursue the Marathas, forcing the last of them into submission in 1818.

In little over fifty years the British had defeated all of the various factions that had grown powerful with the collapse of Mogul power. The final demise of the Marathas left the British in undisputed control of what had been the Mogul Empire. Although the East India Company still paid deference to the Mogul court, which they had taken under their protection in 1803, this was done mainly for political expediency: Through the Moguls, the East India Company was able to oversee its vast holdings without appearing to be directly involved in Indian politics. The Mogul Empire had been reduced to little more than an administrative arm of the East India Company.

The end was particularly bitter. Bahadur Shah II, the last Mogul emperor, who had been given a pension by the British, was deposed and exiled for his complicity in the Indian Mutiny of 1857. From the conquests of Baber and Akbar to the banishment of its last ruler, the empire had risen and fallen in just over three hundred years. It had achieved what no other Moslem empire before it had even seriously attempted—the control of all of northern India and the unification of the Rajput states.

Unable to administer successfully their policies of toleration and reform, the Mogul emperors had, in effect, planted the seeds of their own destruction. The Moguls lost an empire, but their legacy survives in innumerable monuments and works of art— reminders of more triumphant moments in Mogul history. As an inscription from the Red Fort at Delhi proclaims: "If there is a paradise on the face of the earth/It is this, oh! it is this! it is this!"

Photography Credits

Index